The Smoke of Satan

THE SMOKE
OF SATAN

How Corrupt and Cowardly Bishops
Betrayed Christ, His Church, and the Faithful
. . . and What Can Be Done About It

Philip F. Lawler

TAN Books
Charlotte, North Carolina

Unless otherwise noted, Scripture quotations are from the Revised Standard Version of the Bible—Second Catholic Edition (Ignatius Edition), copyright © 2006 National Council of the Churches of Christ in the United States of America. Used by permission. All rights reserved.

Excerpts from the English translation of the Catechism of the Catholic Church for use in the United States of America © 1994, United States Catholic Conference, Inc.—Libreria Editrice Vaticana. Used with permission.

All excerpts from papal homilies, messages, and encyclicals Copyright © Libreria Editrice Vaticana. All rights reserved.

Cover design by Caroline K Green

Cover image: The skullcap of cardinals and bishops, photo by Antonio Nardelli / Shutterstock

ISBN: 978-1-5051-1349-5

Published in the United States by
TAN Books
PO Box 410487
Charlotte, NC 28241
www.TANBooks.com

Printed in the United States of America

Contents

	Publisher's Preface	vii
	Author's Note	xiii
1	The Smoke of Satan	1
2	The Summer of 2018	10
3	The Divisions Revealed	36
4	The Habit of Denial	52
5	With Apologies to the Martyrs	77
6	A Patrimony Squandered	99
7	The Worst of Both Worlds	118
8	The Cultural Revolution: The Enemy Without	137
9	The Limits of Tolerance: The Enemy Within	150
	Conclusion: A Crisis of Leadership	169
	Notes	195
	Sources and Suggestions for Further Reading	199
	About the Author	202

"Philip Lawler is one of the foremost authorities on the Catholic abuse crisis. His new book shows why. With refreshing honesty and deep faith, he describes how sexual, liturgical, and moral abuses intertwine. He also offers practical suggestions for how lay Catholics can respond to the crisis that should be taken to heart by all."

Matthew Schmitz
Senior Editor
First Things

"Phil Lawler saw it coming. On my radio program in the early 90s, Phil predicted that a particular sexual misconduct case under discussion could easily lead to scandal as deep as anything we saw in the 16th century reformation era. He was right. With the summer of McCarrick, Vigano and the PA Grand Jury, the lay faithful are now galvanized as never before to finally take co-responsibility for the Church. Doctrinal disagreements thought settled under the pontificates of John Paul II and Benedict XVI have been reopened. Promises of curial reform and parish renewal have been broken. As a working journalist reporting on all these events for a generation, Phil sees a new Catholic moment for purification and renewal only if we will diagnose how deep the infection goes and stay radically faithful to the Divine Physician whose cure runs deeper still. Read this as a manifesto."

Al Kresta
President and CEO, Ave Maria Communications,
Host, *Kresta in the Afternoon*

Publisher's Preface

You hold in your hands what is, in many ways, the most difficult book we at TAN have published since my family acquired the company in 2008. It is also one of the most important. The recent revelations about Cardinal McCarrick and the publication of the Pennsylvania Report have reminded all Catholics that something remains dreadfully wrong in our beloved Church. Though much progress has been made in the area of sexual abuse prevention and reporting procedures in most dioceses, fundamental problems persist in that area as well as others. The unpleasant truth stares us in the face.

For twelve years, I chaired a Diocesan Review Board for Allegations of Sexual Misconduct Involving Minors. Along with other board members, I have personally spoken with victims and alleged victims and heard their horror stories firsthand. We interviewed accused priests and heard the honest denials of some and the lies of others. We found some allegations to be credible and others not credible. In some cases, we recommended suspension from ministry and laicization, while in other cases, we concluded the allegations to be false and defamatory. We dealt with both civil lawyers and canon lawyers.

On a personal level, the abuse scandal is something I have personally lived since 2002. I know firsthand that many good and honorable bishops have worked diligently to eradicate this sin and this crime of abuse from our Church. The statistics indicate much success has been realized. They should be highly commended. Their efforts and achievements should not be ignored because of the sins of others. Nevertheless, we have recently learned that some bishops were more involved in covering up for abusive priests than we previously knew. These individuals may never fully realize the damage they have caused, but the damage is real and extensive. There are a number of bishops who put the protection of reputations above the protection of children. They should be called to account just as the courageous bishops who did not should be lauded for their fidelity.

Throughout my many years of dealing with the abuse issue, I have asked myself what is the cause. I long ago concluded that sexual abuse was a symptom of a diabolical influence that entered the Church, the "smoke of Satan" to which Pope Saint Paul VI referred, for abuse and cover-ups on a scale that we have seen do not just spring forth from a healthy organization. Something beyond the abusive conduct itself must be at work.

In the following pages, noted Catholic journalist and author Phil Lawler demonstrates that what has occurred in the past fifty plus years in the Catholic Church constitutes nothing less than a massive betrayal: first and foremost, the betrayal of the poor souls sexually abused by men they looked to as spiritual fathers, but a betrayal in many other ways as well. Principally, what Lawler argues is that many bishops have betrayed God and the faithful by failing to, in season and out of season, fulfill the three fundamental duties of their office: to teach, to sanctify, and to govern.

The Betrayal of the Duty to Teach

While much progress was made following the publication of the *Catechism of the Catholic Church*, Catholics would have to have their heads in the sand to ignore the fact that a widespread ignorance of basic Catholic teaching remains the norm rather than the exception among much of the laity. The clearest indicator of this, as Lawler emphasizes, are the depressing statistics—both "official" in the form of studies, and anecdotal in the form of just taking a look around—of how many Catholics use birth control in their marriage.

One would rather not so often point to sexual sins as examples, and, perhaps sadly, we need not do so, for examples of a fundamental ignorance of or confusion about basic Catholic doctrine among the laity is all too obvious . . . again both statistically and anecdotally. Anecdotally, perhaps the strongest evidence is the fact that, in most American parishes, everyone or almost everyone receives communion every Sunday. And yet, if you visited the confession line on the Saturday afternoon when it is usually offered, you would see the priest and perhaps a small number of penitents, maybe one or two or three. That fact alone betrays a fundamental ignorance of the sacramental economy. The first duty of the priest is to bring Christ to the people and the people to Christ . . . in a phrase, to save souls. The "ordinary" way in which a Catholic priest does so is through hearing the sins of the penitent and granting God's absolution. Why are not more priests in the confessional before every daily Mass as

mine is? Why do not more bishops insist that they be there?
As any priest who offers frequent opportunities for confession can tell you: "Offer it and they will come."

The Betrayal of the Duty to Sanctify

Lawler's chapter titled *With Apologies to the Martyrs* asks the
question, *What was different?* What inspired so many of the
faithful in past centuries to abandon their homes and their
families and go to distant lands to bring the gospel, to bring
Christ and salvation, to strangers. What kind of homilies did
they hear? What so impressed them that they recognized their
own salvation was intimately connected to how radically they
were willing to follow Christ in the love of God and neighbor.
A bishop's duty is to sanctify, his entire flock to be sure, but
in a special way his duty is to sanctify his priests, who then, in
turn, bring God's healing and grace to a suffering world. We
do have, today, a number of good and holy priests and bishops, on fire for the faith; however, we also see a number that
seem apathetic about their solemn responsibilities or are too
timid to carry them out, or, horrible to note, seem not to hold
the Catholic Faith at all. There was a wonderful book published a number of years ago by Father George Rutler entitled *A Crisis of Saints*. When the bishops fail to sanctify their
flock, but most especially their priests, that crisis, which in
one sense can be considered the only crisis which ever afflicts
the Church, will be all too evident. We need saints.

The Betrayal of the Duty to Govern

Here we can see a failure in two different ways. Many heterodox bishops have governed their dioceses effectively, with an

iron hand one might say, and they have destroyed or nearly destroyed the Faith in those places for generations. And, sadly, too many good bishops have failed to adequately bring their dioceses under their control. They preside over a school system that fails to teach the Catholic faith, a chancery populated by dissidents, and, despite their own personal orthodoxy, lack the strength of will to truly govern as they should. Governance requires a strong hand and a willingness to make hard decisions and, yes, to be unliked. Too many bishops, good men in and of themselves and, again, personally orthodox, maybe even holy, seem to have forgotten Christ's words: *When you are persecuted for my sake . . .* (cf. Mt 5:11).

A Final Note

Concerned Catholics can disagree on the extent to which individual bishops are culpable for participating in a sort of collegial club, one in which one never speaks ill of another. You will note, as you read this book, that Phil Lawler takes a very hard line on the question. Even within our offices here at TAN, there are differing opinions as to how much responsibility bishops as individuals bear (With regards to Cardinal McCarrick, one wonders of each man: What did he know and when did he know it?), but without any doubt, just as the priesthood itself has been grievously damaged by the small percentage of abusers within its ranks, so too the bishops, as a body, have been grievously damaged by the corruption and weakness of their brother bishops. Their teaching and moral authority, again, principally as a body, but also individually, will take years to restore. Sadly, the Spanish adage, "los justos pagan por pecadores" applies. The just pay for sinners. What the depravity of so many priests and the cowardice or heterodoxy of so many bishops have wrought in God's Church, and done to their own good names, should outrage the holy and orthodox bishops and priests among us.

Here at TAN, we know that there are many bishops reinvigorating their dioceses and carrying out their duties to teach, sanctify, and govern their local Churches. We do not want to tar all bishops with the same brush, but we are not doing the tarring . . . that dirty job has been done. The smoke of Satan has, as Pope Saint Paul VI declared over forty years ago, truly entered the sanctuary. It manifests itself both in the disgusting and depraved actions of those priests and bishops and cardinals who have figured so much in the news, but also in the spirit of cowardice that has affected, no, infected too many who, on the day of their ordination, pledged to lay down their lives for Jesus Christ. Only each individual priest and bishop can look into his own heart and know the truth of his own soul, the times he was courageous and the times he was cowardly. We at TAN want to assure those bishops—imperfect as are we all—who truly seek to do God's will that they can have no firmer ally than TAN Books and Saint Benedict Press. Let us go forth together in truth, identify the problems and their causes, and begin the hard work of rebuilding God's Church together.

Robert M. Gallagher, President & CEO
On behalf of TAN Books/Saint Benedict Press
October 22, 2018
Feast of Pope Saint John Paul II

Author's Note

This book has been written during a time of intense discussion and debate within the Catholic Church, especially in the United States. I have written quickly—in a bid to influence that discussion—and so I do not have the option of waiting until all arguments have been heard, all claims and counter-claims settled. There will be new revelations and new developments, no doubt, between the time when I finish writing (in early October 2018) and the time when this book appears—and then the prospect of many more new developments, perhaps for years, until the current crisis is resolved. Readers who are interested in my reactions to the latest developments will find my commentary on the Catholic Culture website (www.catholicculture.org), where I post several times a week.

Chapter 1

The Smoke of Satan

In Jerusalem, just outside the walled Old City, stands the church of St. Peter in Gallicantu: St. Peter as the Cock Crows. Catholic churches are regularly dedicated to saints, but only rarely to a particular moment in a saint's life. Then again, this is no ordinary saint, no ordinary moment.

St. Peter in Gallicantu was built in the fifth century, and rebuilt by Crusaders, on the spot traditionally thought to have been the site where Caiaphas the high priest lived, where Jesus was brought to stand trial. In the courtyard of that house, Peter three times denied that he was a follower of Christ. The Gospel of Luke (22:60–62) recounts the incident: "And immediately, while he was still speaking, the cock crowed. And the Lord turned and looked at Peter. And Peter remembered the word of the Lord, how he had said to him, 'Before the cock crows today, you will deny me three times.' And he went out and wept bitterly."

In his tears—in his repentance, his willingness to throw himself on Christ's mercy—Peter found redemption. The first pope, the acknowledged hero and leader of the early Christian community, was, and knew himself to be, a flawed man.

Nor was Peter the only one of Christ's followers to desert him in his time of trial. Of the twelve apostles, the Gospel accounts put only John at the foot of the Cross, keeping vigil with Jesus; the others were not on the scene. Of course, John was not alone. With him was Mary, the Mother of Jesus, who, unlike the apostles, was not flawed and never deserted her Son.

"The Church on earth," the Second Vatican Council proclaimed, "is endowed already with a sanctity that is real though imperfect" (*Lumen Gentium* 48). The *Catechism of the Catholic Church*, after quoting that sentence, continues, "In her members perfect holiness is something yet to be acquired" (825).

When the cock crowed, Peter painfully recognized his sinfulness, his need to acquire holiness: a need that he felt through the day of his martyrdom. For Mary—who, the Church teaches, was born without stain of sin—holiness was and is a constant. In that respect, Mary is a model of the Church: always faithful, the spotless Bride of Christ. But Peter and the apostles are also a model of the Church: the hierarchical institution, founded by Christ, guided by the Holy Spirit, yet confided into the care of fallen men.

For Catholics, it is always a challenge to keep these two models of the Church in proper perspective. The mystical, Marian model, without the practical guidance of the teaching hierarchy, can veer off into emotionalism and amorphous sentimentality. The Petrine model, stripped of the

Marian warmth, can become cold and calculating. In *The Beauty of Holiness and the Holiness of Beauty*, John Saward writes, "Detached from Mary, the Church is no longer seen as a person, a woman, Christ's bride, and our mother, but as an organization, a conspiracy of interfering clergymen." And, one might add, that is, in fact, what it becomes.

The faithful Catholic should recognize Christ's Church in both models, Marian and Petrine. Toward the Marian Church the appropriate attitude is a childlike trust and devotion. Toward the Petrine Church, a mature adult's confidence.

But what happens when the members of the hierarchy, the leaders of the Petrine Church, lose our confidence? It can happen; they are ordinary humans with ordinary weaknesses. And often they face the extraordinary temptation to substitute their own judgment for the guidance of the Holy Spirit. When St. Peter voiced his own personal opinion that Jesus should not be given up to death, the Lord rebuked him severely: "Get behind me, Satan! You are a hindrance to me; for you are not on the side of God, but of men" (Mt 16:23).

The history of the Catholic Church is a history marked by success and failure, by sanctity and by sin, by splendor and by corruption. This of course is the history of the visible Church, the hierarchical model; through it all, the Marian Church remains pure and loyal. In good times and bad, the sacraments are administered, the Eucharist is celebrated; Christ is with his Church, offering salvation. The invisible work of the Church is always the first priority. Frank Sheed remarked in *Christ in Eclipse*, "We are not baptized into the hierarchy, do not receive the cardinals sacramentally, will not spend eternity in the beatific vision of the Pope. . . . Christ is the point."

Still, it is wrong to dismiss the importance of the hierarchy. Jesus promised that the Holy Spirit would guide the Church always, that despite the manifest weaknesses of her leaders, the Church would prevail over the gates of hell. Popes and bishops have made innumerable errors of judgment over the course of generations, yet the Church still survives, the faith still spreads, while other once-powerful human institutions wither and die. The very fact that the Church has weathered all storms, regardless of the helmsmen's errors, is in itself evidence of the Spirit's power. As Hilaire Belloc famously quipped, the "Catholic Church is an institution I am bound to hold divine—but for unbelievers a proof of its divinity might be found in the fact that no merely human institution conducted with such knavish imbecility would have lasted a fortnight."

Knavish imbecility: those are harsh words. But in 2018, loyal Catholics are using that sort of language, and worse, to describe the shocking malfeasance of bishops, especially in response to the sex-abuse scandal. Our bishops have betrayed our trust; a deep and pervasive corruption within the hierarchy has been exposed. As a chastened Archbishop Thomas Wenski of Miami observed in a September homily, "Our people still do believe in God; but they don't believe in us."[1]

How did our bishops lose the confidence of the faithful, and how can the profound damage to the Church be repaired? This book is written in an effort to answer those questions.

On one level, the first question can be answered quite

simply. The bishops lost our confidence because, as a group, they were—and were shown to be—dishonest. They covered up evidence of sexual abuse and misled the public with claims that the problem had been resolved. Still worse, their dishonesty continued even after their negligence had been painfully, thoroughly exposed. Even conscientious bishops, whose own conduct and leadership were beyond reproach, contributed to the overall problem by failing to denounce those who were flagrantly corrupt and dishonest. The same sort of cover-ups that shocked the faithful when they were brought to light in 2002 were unearthed once again in 2018, and this time, the faithful, having been assured that the bishops had learned their lessons, were outraged to learn that the deceit had continued.

Somehow bishops had become convinced that by suppressing the truth about clerical misconduct, they were serving the Church. Obviously, something had gone terribly wrong with their understanding of the Church they served; the Marian model was missing. Can anyone imagine the Virgin Mary telling lies? Tolerating the abuse of children? Allowing predators to serve on the altar, performing sacred rites? Certainly not; the mere suggestion is repugnant.

Why, then, did our bishops and other Church leaders not instantly recognize the grave moral wrong that was done when they failed to do all in their power to expose, punish, and prevent abuse? That tolerance for evil was, alas, not an isolated phenomenon. The second outcropping of the scandal, in 2018, showed that the same ugly attitudes were the norm rather than the exception across hundreds of dioceses and dozens of countries, and even at the Vatican. Nor was this a problem that arose under Pope Francis; the historical evidence stretched back for decades, tarring the records of his predecessors.

This habit of dishonesty, I will argue, has been built up in the Catholic hierarchy through years of avoiding conflicts, managing the control of information, and preserving appearances—all motivated by a powerful desire to avoid confronting some fundamental problems. To preserve a façade of unity, bishops have deliberately ignored deep divisions among the faithful: divisions on matters of theological doctrine, moral practice, and canonical discipline. As a result of this negligence, over the years Catholic doctrine has become blurred, moral practice lax, and discipline within the ranks virtually non-existent.

Back in 1972, on the ninth anniversary of his installation as Roman pontiff, Pope Paul VI recognized the problems that had sprung up throughout the universal Church in the wake of the Second Vatican Council: "the rising tide of profanity, of desacralization, of secularization that wants to confuse and overwhelm the religious sense in the secret of the heart, in private life, or even in the affirmations of public life." These ills were not coming exclusively from outside the Church; Pope Paul warned, "Through some fissure the smoke of Satan has entered the temple of God." He spoke of "something preternatural that has come into the world precisely to disturb, to suffocate the fruits of the ecumenical council."[2]

In that sobering statement, Pope Paul acknowledged that the Church in the late twentieth century faced a rising tide of secularization. But he saw a more sinister threat as well: a diabolical assault on the integrity of the Faith. Is it unreasonable to think of the sex-abuse scandal as a show of the devil's success? Could there be any more effective way to undermine the authority of the Church than to show that priests had molested children and bishops had allowed the abuse to continue unchecked?

Pope Paul's evocative image of the "smoke of Satan" also suggested that the atmosphere within the Church had been tainted, that vision had been obscured, so that pastors no longer saw issues clearly. And sad to say, although he acknowledged the danger, Pope Paul was unable to avert it. The secular tide kept rising, while the divisions within the Catholic community grew wider.

***

"Our enemy today is the world: the spirit of the world," Archbishop Fulton Sheen, the great Catholic evangelist, said in a memorable television address in 1974. He went on to recall that ten or twenty years earlier, it had been much easier to live a Christian life in America: "The atmosphere was Christian; morals were Christian; there was not a great problem in adapting ourselves to a Christian society. But now, when everything is turned around, these are days when the masks have come off, and we reveal ourselves just as we really are."[3]

And what are we, really? Have we, as Catholic Christians, preserved our faith, our way of life, in an increasingly secular culture? Or has the culture sapped the evangelical energy of the Church? The Second Vatican Council was convened by Pope John XXIII to provide guidance on how the

Church could meet the challenges of a secular culture. In that regard, at least, the promise of the council has clearly been unfulfilled.

What were "the fruits of the ecumenical council," which Pope Paul saw endangered? Some theologians and commentators, on the "progressive" wing of the Church, welcomed Vatican II as a sharp break with Catholic tradition, an invitation to an entirely new approach to the Faith. Others, more conservative (and more faithful to the actual documents produced by the council), saw it as a re-affirmation of traditional teachings, combined with a new pastoral approach. Still others, on the "traditionalist" wing, agreed with the "progressives" that the council had been a radical break, but lamented it.

Pope John Paul II, who had been an influential participant in the council deliberations, sought to reconcile the opposing factions, but with limited success. Pope Benedict XVI, the greatest Catholic theologian of his generation, taught that the work of Vatican II must be interpreted using a "hermeneutic of continuity" so that the council's documents were read in the perspective of the Church's constant teaching. But while these two great pontiffs gave the Church a rich treasury of teaching, they could not root out the disagreements among the faithful. The divisions within the Church remained; the arguments over fundamental beliefs raged on.

To avoid bitter clashes, Church leaders—including those two popes—did their best to downplay the differences among the faithful, to paper over the divisions. So when theologians at Catholic universities denied what the popes affirmed, they were rarely corrected. When priests violated liturgical norms, they were rarely rebuked. Mass attendance plummeted, priests and religious by the thousands abandoned their vocations, parochial schools closed, and yet Church leaders avoided expressions of urgency and crisis.

To advance through the ranks of the hierarchy in the late twentieth century, clerics were expected to suppress problems rather than confront them, to soothe the faithful rather than rouse them, to conceal problems rather than admit them. In that atmosphere, when bishops learned that priests had molested young men, they did their best to "manage" the issue, to keep things running smoothly, above all to avoid calling public attention to the problem. So the abuse continued—just as the theological dissent and the liturgical abuse continued. But finally, as almost always happens, the cover-up failed; the truth of the abuse scandal emerged. Now that the evidence that was suppressed for decades has exploded into public view, the bishops' neglect—likely too benign a word—is unmistakable.

If the fundamental problem facing the Church is dishonesty—a habit of deliberate ambiguity, a failure to grapple with hard truths—then the solution must be a candid, unapologetic return to the truth: not only in addressing and dealing with the shocking details of clerical abuse, but also in the proclamation of the truths of the Catholic faith. And if the bishops have lost their instinct for that forthright evangelical approach, then it falls upon lay Catholics—in this era, proclaimed by Vatican II as "the age of the laity"—to demand the truth and reclaim the Catholic tradition.

CHAPTER 2

The Summer of 2018

Every five hundred years, it seems, Christianity faces some historic crisis that changes the face of the Church: the fall of the Roman Empire, the Great Schism, the Protestant Reformation. The crisis that is upon us now, the clash between faith and materialism, has been building for decades, and its final outcome is uncertain. But when historians write about the great cultural contest of the twenty-first century, they might well say that the crisis peaked in the United States during the summer of 2018.

The year began quietly enough. In January, when Pope Francis delivered the traditional papal "State of the World" address to the Vatican diplomatic corps, the pontiff spoke about the environment, immigration, and human rights. In Rome, the liveliest theological debates still revolved around *Amoris Laetitia*, the controversial document on marriage that Pope Francis had released nearly two full years earlier. There were rumors that the Vatican might soon strike a deal with the government of China, allowing the Communist regime a say in the appointment of bishops. (The aging Cardinal Joseph Zen, retired archbishop of Hong Kong, stood quietly in the cold rain during a January papal audience, waiting for a chance to present the pope with a petition begging him to reconsider any such deal with Beijing.) Vatican journalists scarcely mentioned the sex-abuse problem.

But January 2018 also brought a papal visit to Chile, where the stage was set for a searing drama. The Catholic community in Chile had been stunned in 2015 when the pope appointed Bishop Juan Barros to head the Osorno diocese. Bishop Barros had been closely associated with Father Fernando Karadima, a once phenomenally popular priest in Chile who, it was revealed, had sexually abused a number of young men, and the appointment stirred up popular protests. Priests of the Osorno diocese refused to accept the new bishop; even Chilean bishops questioned the pope's selection. But Francis stood his ground, insisting that there was no evidence that Barros had been aware of Karadima's crimes.

Greeted by protesters in Chile, the pope adamantly defended the unpopular bishop. He concelebrated Mass with Bishop Barros; he told reporters that the charges against the bishop were "calumny." He said, "There is not a single proof against him." Repeating that the bishop's critics were guilty of calumny, the pope said, "I cannot condemn him without evidence."[4]

This blithe dismissal of public concerns was too much for even stalwart supporters of the pontiff. Cardinal Sean O'Malley of Boston, the chairman of a special papal commission on sexual abuse, said that the pope's remarks were a "source of great pain for survivors of sexual abuse."[5] The secular press, which had favored Pope Francis with remarkably positive coverage, began investigating the story in Chile, taking note of the close connections between Barros and Karadima. At first, reporters remained favorably disposed toward the pontiff; a February story from the Associated Press explored the possibility that the difficulties in Chile arose because the pope's aides had not properly informed him about the situation. But within a few weeks, that hypothesis was rejected. The Associated Press learned that the pope had received a letter from one of Karadima's victims, delivered by Cardinal O'Malley, explaining in detail how Barros had been aware of—if not personally involved with—Karadima's crimes.[6]

Thrust abruptly onto the defensive, the Vatican defended the pope's commitment to curbing clerical abuse. The Vatican press office announced that the pontiff had been speaking with abuse victims "several times a month," without ever allowing any public mention of the meetings. The pope named new members to the papal abuse commission, issuing a new statement of determination to protect children. But even that move prompted critical comments because the commission's mandate had quietly expired a few months earlier, an apparent indication that it was not a top papal priority.

It was then that the pope's public-relations problems began to multiply. In March, the Vatican publicized a letter from pope-emeritus Benedict XVI commenting on the "interior continuity" between his leadership and that of Pope Francis. The letter was made public as the Vatican released a series of booklets on the theology of Pope Francis. The publications were obviously intended to bolster the pontiff's image as a theologian, and the letter from Benedict was designed to discourage the grumbling by conservative Catholics who saw the new pope's policies as a radical break from those of his predecessors.

But a veteran Italian journalist, Sandro Magister of *L'Espresso*, dug a bit deeper into the story and revealed that the letter from Benedict was actually not an endorsement of the new pope's approach. On the contrary, when he had been asked by Msgr. Dario Vigano (to be distinguished from Carlo Maria Vigano, who has figured so much in the news and who will be mentioned at length later in this book) to comment on the booklets, Benedict had declined even to read them, offering the polite but unconvincing excuse that he was too busy. Undeterred, Msgr. Vigano—the prefect of the Vatican's Secretariat for Communications—read aloud from Benedict's letter at a press conference introducing the new books, giving reporters the impression that the retired pope had endorsed the project. He even distributed a photographic copy of Benedict's letter. But as the journalist Magister pointed out, the copy had been doctored so that the paragraph in which Benedict declined to read the volumes was illegible.[7]

Altering a photo is a clear violation of journalistic standards, and reporters did not react kindly when they learned that they had been hoodwinked. So the transparent bid to generate favorable coverage for the pope backfired, bringing on a new spate of adverse publicity. Msgr. Vigano was forced to resign from his post as the head of the Vatican's communications machinery—although he was allowed to remain as a consultant to the office, in a sign of continued papal favor.

For the first time, mainstream reporters began making critical remarks about the pope's statements and policies and noticing indications that the pontiff and his aides were facing resistance from within the hierarchy. When Francis released a new apostolic exhortation, *Gaudete et Exsultate*, on the quest for personal holiness, a *New York Times* report commented that the pope was "pushing back against conservative critics within the Church."[8]

Meanwhile, in a belated response to the uproar in Chile, the pope had sent Archbishop Charles Scicluna, formerly the Vatican's top prosecutor of sex-abuse cases, to investigate the situation. After scores of interviews with prelates and abuse victims, the archbishop returned with a voluminous and thoroughly damning report. "I have made serious mistakes in the assessment and perception of the situation," Pope Francis confessed, attributing his failure to "the lack of truthful and balanced information."

Tensions mounted at the Vatican in May, and not only because the pope had summoned the bishops of Chile for a discussion of their crisis. Before they arrived, the Catholic bishops of Germany gathered in Rome to pursue a different debate. The German bishops' conference had drafted a policy that would allow the non-Catholic spouses of Catholics to receive Communion on a regular basis. When a minority of German bishops objected, the dispute was referred to the Vatican's Congregation for the Doctrine of the Faith (CDF). After meeting with the German delegation, Archbishop Luis

Ladaria, the CDF prefect, disclosed that the pope would not issue a ruling on the matter; he hoped that the German bishops would resolve the disagreement by themselves. (Eventually they did—more or less. The bishops' conference quietly published the policy, without giving it any official approval, thus encouraging the expanded approach to intercommunion without ever resolving the concerns of those who said the policy was a clear violation of canon law.)

On May 5, with the Chilean bishops' arrival still ten days in the future, the focus shifted back to the sex-abuse issue. That Sunday, Pope Francis presided at a Mass celebrating the fiftieth anniversary of the lay movement, the Neocatechumenal Way. There on the stage, in a place of honor close to the pontiff, was Archbishop Anthony Apuron from Guam. Archbishop Apuron had been a friend of the Neocatechumenal Way. But he had been convicted by a Vatican tribunal on charges related to sexual abuse and removed from his archdiocese. True, he had appealed the sentence and still proclaimed his innocence, but after he had been charged—not merely with ignoring evidence of abuse but with molesting boys himself—and stripped of his pastoral office, why would he be given a prominent role in a papal ceremony just weeks after his conviction had been announced?[9]

In mid-May, when the Chilean bishops arrived, the scene was quiet for a few days, then exploded with the unprecedented news that all thirty-one active diocesan bishops in Chile had offered their resignations. Although the Chilean prelates said that they were acting on their own initiative, it was difficult to imagine that they could have taken such a dramatic action without at least the implicit approval of the Holy Father. Their willingness to step down *en masse*, whether or not it was prompted by a papal demand, was a clear signal that, in the eyes of the Vatican, the corruption exposed by the scandal in Chile had penetrated deep enough that the entire episcopal conference had forfeited its credibility and direct papal intervention was required.

However, the Chilean bishops' resignations came without any further explanation, any public analysis of where the prelates had gone wrong. The resignations were left on the pope's desk, to be accepted or not. And when Pope Francis gradually began to accept some of the resignations, he did not explain why those particular bishops were being removed while others remained in office. Even when he finally accepted the resignation of the notorious Bishop Barros, nearly a month later, the pope offered no comment.

By handing the pontiff the power to remove bishops at will, without explanation, the Chilean hierarchy had opened a new chapter in this unusual papacy. For all his talk of collegial government and decentralized ecclesiastical power, Pope Francis was now openly making unilateral decisions on the fitness of individual diocesan bishops. That surprising expansion of the pope's prerogative could have implications for ecumenical relations; Orthodox prelates, already leery of papal authority, could fear that any vestige of their autonomy would be lost if they entered into communion with the Holy See.

Moreover, the pope's decisions on which resignations to accept, made without public explanation, left observers wondering about one prominent Chilean prelate who had *not* resigned. Cardinal Francisco Javier Errázuriz had already stepped down as Archbishop of Santiago. But he remained an active member of the Council of Cardinals, the pope's top advisory board. And Cardinal Errázuriz had acknowledged that he delayed for five years before investigating abuse charges against Karadima; later he had urged Vatican officials not to hear testimony from Karadima's most prominent accuser. While the cardinal had denied deliberately covering up Karadima's crimes, even the most benign view of his actions (or inaction) showed him to have been woefully negligent. So it was not surprising that he did not travel to Rome for the May meeting; it seemed inevitable that he would be quietly dropped from the Council of Cardinals. But he was not. His advanced age (he is now eighty-five) as well as his unfortunate role in the Karadima affair would seem to give compelling reasons for his replacement on the pope's top advisory board. Yet to this day he remains an official member.

But in June, the pope *did* remove a prominent cardinal from office. And when he did, any hope for the usual quiet summer in Rome was dashed.

On June 20, Cardinal Theodore McCarrick, the retired Archbishop of Washington, DC, issued a statement indicating that he would cease public ministry because of a complaint of sexual abuse. Cardinal Timothy Dolan of New York, who had supervised an investigation at the Vatican's request, announced that a review board "found the allegations credible and substantiated."[10] McCarrick protested his innocence and said that he had "absolutely no recollection of this reported abuse" but accepted the pope's ruling that he should confine himself to "a life of prayer and penance."[11] In July, he formally resigned his position as a cardinal.

The complaint against McCarrick involved a young man, a legal minor. But after he was deposed, multiple witnesses came forward to report that the former cardinal had long been notorious for taking seminarians to bed at his beach house on the New Jersey shore. The seminarians were not minors, and so McCarrick's sexual activities were not illegal, nor did they violate the American bishops' sex-abuse policies. But the fact that a cardinal had been actively homosexual, and his colleagues had taken no action, was another damaging blow to the credibility of the hierarchy.[12]

In November 2003, during a PBS interview, Cardinal Dolan had responded emphatically to a question about whether the bishops' vigilance regarding sexual misconduct might fade over time: "Can't happen. Can't happen. We never, never, Kim, want to go through what we've had to do. We just can't do it. We can't do it personally. I think we bishops will collapse if we ever have to go through this again. And we can't, we just can't, in justice, put our people through that again."

As June 2018 drew to a close, it was clear: the American bishops were putting their people through it again.

And not only the American bishops. The echoes of the Chilean debacle were still resounding around St. Peter's Square in July when the Vatican announced the resignation of Bishop Juan José Pineda Fasquelle, the vicar general of the Archdiocese of Tegucigalpa, Honduras. Bishop Pineda, too, had been accused of molesting seminarians; in fact, a group of fifty seminarians from Honduras had issued an open letter claiming "irrefutable evidence" of a homosexual network in the archdiocese. Their charges were especially noteworthy because the Archbishop of Tegucigalpa was Cardinal Óscar Rodríguez Maradiaga, the chairman of the pope's Council of Cardinals. And so another member of the pope's top advisory board had been tainted by the scandal.

In August—traditionally the quietest month of the year at the Vatican, when Church officials abandon Rome for cooler climes—the spotlight shifted briefly away from the sex-abuse scandal when Pope Francis ordered a change in the *Catechism of the Catholic Church*, saying that the death penalty is "inadmissible" in light of the Gospel and that the Church "works with determination for its abolition worldwide." The Church has traditionally taught that the state has the right to use capital punishment when necessary. Granted, the language in the *Catechism* promulgated by John Paul II included the caveat—itself a quote from his encyclical *Evangelium Vitae* (56)—that the circumstances in which the state may have recourse to the death penalty are "very rare, if not practically non-existent" (CCC 2267). But this new statement seemed to eliminate the idea that the state could, even in principle, be justified in executing a criminal; the new text of the *Catechism* offered no authority other than Pope Francis himself for this apparent change in teaching. But the revised text proclaimed, "A new understanding has emerged of the significance of penal sanctions imposed by the state." The text did not explain what that "new understanding" might be, nor did it explain why a moral *principle*—the potential justice of execution—could be based on a prudential judgment, which could change with time.

However, any incipient debate on the morality of capital punishment, or the difference between an "inadmissible" act and one that is "intrinsically" immoral, was soon drowned out by stunning new developments on the sex-abuse front, coming on consecutive days at the end of August.

On August 14, the Commonwealth of Pennsylvania released a devastating grand-jury report on sexual abuse within the Church, covering seventy years of clerical misconduct. The report was heart-rending; the details were appalling. There were hundreds of cases in which priests molested children, and when bishops failed to take effective action, the children were molested again. Some of the abuse was gruesome almost beyond belief: groups of priests who passed around their young partners, rapists who forced their victims to pose on crosses in a bizarre parody of the Crucifixion that suggested satanic involvement. For anyone who had lived through the "long Lent" of 2002, and had read the details of cases that came to light at that time, the pattern of the bishops' response was sadly familiar. In one case after another, bishops shuffled the predators from one parish to another, helping them to avoid detection. Although thousands of criminal acts were reported by the grand jury, there were no prosecutions planned; the statute of limitations protected the accused priests—if they were still alive.

The vast majority of the cases covered by the Pennsylvania report were taken from before the American bishops instituted their "Dallas Charter" policies for punishing clerical abuse, and the report indicated a sharp decrease in abuse since 2002. But the damage was done. The public was rocked by another detailed, undeniable litany of clerical misconduct and episcopal negligence. Even if in most cases the negligent bishops were deceased or at least retired, it remained true that their successors, the bishops now heading the Pennsylvania dioceses, had not yet acknowledged the magnitude of past offenses. So the revelations could be, and often were, taken as another stark reminder that the American Catholic bishops could not be trusted to protect their people.

Just eleven days after the release of the Pennsylvania grand-jury report, a former Vatican diplomat issued his own stunning testimony. Archbishop Carlo Maria Viganò, who had served as apostolic nuncio in Washington (that is, the equivalent of the Vatican's ambassador to the US), disclosed that Pope Francis had been aware of McCarrick's sexual misconduct for at least five years and nonetheless had made the American prelate "the kingmaker" for appointments in the Curia and the United States, the most listened-to adviser in the Vatican on relations with the Obama administration. Archbishop Viganò also said that Pope Benedict XVI, having heard of McCarrick's escapades, had imposed sanctions on the American prelate, instructing him to remove himself from public life.

Archbishop Viganò wrote bluntly about "homosexual networks" at the Vatican, saying that they were responsible for the advancement of some prelates. He named names. In Rome, he said, Cardinal Francesco Coccopalmerio (the former head of the Vatican's top dicastery for interpreting canon law) and Archbishop Vincenzo Paglia (the current president of the Pontifical Academy for Life) were part of "the homosexual current in favor of subverting Catholic doctrine on homosexuality." In the United States, he said,

Cardinals Joseph Tobin of Newark and Blase Cupich of Chicago had received their red hats because of the influence of a homosexual network within the clergy, a force that had come to be known as the "lavender mafia."

The former Vatican diplomat alluded to reports that Cardinal Sean O'Malley of Boston, the chairman of the papal sex-abuse commission, had received warning about McCarrick's activities in 2015 but had taken no action. Cardinal O'Malley had responded to the criticism, saying that the letter addressed to him by a prominent New York priest had been opened and reviewed by his staff, and since the complaint against McCarrick did not involve a minor, his aides concluded that the problem did not lie in Cardinal O'Malley's jurisdiction.[13]

Cardinal O'Malley was also a member of the Council of Cardinals, and so the name of a third member of that body had been mentioned in the context of these revelations. A fourth member, Cardinal George Pell, was already facing criminal charges in his native Australia for alleged sexual abuse forty years ago; although the charges were questionable and the cardinal has consistently proclaimed his innocence, still the fact remains that four of the nine members of the pope's "cabinet" (O'Malley, Pell, Errázuriz, and Maradiaga) had been drawn into yet another scandal rocking the Petrine Church.

Archbishop Viganò's remarkable letter hit Church leaders like a thunderbolt. Never before had a veteran Curial official made such a detailed charge against top Vatican officials, including the pope himself. The archbishop, in his eleven-page broadside, had also implicated three Vatican

Secretaries of State—Cardinals Angelo Sodano, Tarcisio Bertone, and the incumbent, Pietro Parolin—in the cover-up of abuse.

If the Viganò testimony was accurate, the Vatican administration was thoroughly corrupt. "If Viganò is telling the truth about these things," wrote Sohrab Ahmari in the *New York Post*, "then the moral catastrophe he describes is horrifyingly real. Everything else is noise."[14] But was the testimony accurate? At several points in his bombshell testimony, Archbishop Viganò explained where the corroborating evidence could be found: in files at the Vatican or the offices of the apostolic nuncio. If those files were made public—or even vetted by a reliable, objective investigator—the world would soon know whether the archbishop's remarkable account was accurate. But the Vatican showed no inclination to open those files. Instead, defenders of the pontiff attacked Archbishop Viganò's motives, saying that his letter was part of a partisan attack on the Holy Father.

Pope Francis himself was almost entirely silent about the Viganò testimony. Questioned by reporters, he made an uncharacteristic announcement that "I will not say a single word about this." Instead he challenged the reporters: "Read the statement carefully and make your own judgment."

The pope's defenders took a more active approach, however. They reminded reporters that Archbishop Viganò had clashed with other officials at the Vatican during his tenure there, and his appointment to the diplomatic post in Washington had been seen as a sort of exile. Now he was taking his revenge, they hinted. They pointed out that McCarrick had been seen in public quite frequently after the time when

Pope Benedict had supposedly consigned him to a private life; in fact, Archbishop Viganò himself had joined in ceremonies with the disgraced cardinals. Still the pope's men did not—apparently could not—deny the basic facts contained in the archbishop's charge.

Even someone inclined to believe the Viganò testimony was forced to acknowledge that on several points, his account of the McCarrick scandal seemed inconsistent with known facts. But on each point, there was a plausible explanation for the inconsistency:

Inconsistency 1: the "secret sanctions"

- Archbishop Viganò reported that Pope Benedict XVI restricted McCarrick's ministry. But there was no public evidence of any such disciplinary action.
- *Explanation*: Pope Benedict imposed the restrictions secretly.
- Is that explanation consistent with Pope Benedict's track record? Yes.

Earlier in his pontificate, Pope Benedict had restricted Father Marcial Maciel to a life of prayer and penance but made no announcement of that action. The disciplinary action became public knowledge only after the fact. McCarrick was already retired, so there was no need to remove him from office; he could simply have been ordered to keep a low profile.

Inconsistency 2: McCarrick's public appearances

- In fact, McCarrick did *not* keep a low profile. He did move out of a seminary, and at least one major appearance was cancelled. But he appeared at many other public events.
- *Explanation*: McCarrick simply ignored the pope's directives.
- Is that explanation consistent with the former cardinal's track record? Yes.

In 2004, when the US bishops were engaged in a heated debate about whether politicians who promote abortion should be allowed to receive Communion, Cardinal McCarrick—who had been appointed to chair a special committee on the subject—reported that then-Cardinal Ratzinger had said, in a private letter, that individual bishops should decide the question for their own dioceses. In fact, the letter from Cardinal Ratzinger had stated quite clearly that pro-abortion politicians should be denied the Eucharist. In 2009, at a burial service for Senator Ted Kennedy, McCarrick read a laudatory letter from the Vatican Secretary of State, deliberately creating the impression that it was a message from Pope Benedict, who in fact had studiously avoided any public comment. Clearly the American prelate was willing to flout the wishes of Pope Benedict.

Inconsistency 3: the lack of enforcement

- Although he reports that he told Washington's Cardinal Wuerl not to allow public appearances by McCarrick, Archbishop Viganò apparently did not enforce any papal sanctions. In fact, he himself appeared at public events along with McCarrick.

- *Explanation*: As an archbishop, Viganò did not have the authority to issue orders to a cardinal. And as papal nuncio, he reported to the Vatican Secretary of State. Archbishop Viganò reports that the Secretariat of State protected McCarrick.
- Is that explanation consistent with the track record of the Secretariat of State? Yes.

Particularly under Cardinal Angelo Sodano, the Secretariat of State was notorious for protecting Father Maciel. Like Maciel, McCarrick was an extremely successful fundraiser, who used his prowess to curry favor with the most powerful Vatican officials. Although Cardinal Sodano had retired by the time McCarrick was reportedly disciplined, he remained influential, and according to Archbishop Viganò, his successor, Cardinal Tarcisio Bertone, took a similar line.

Inconsistency 4: the pope's reliance on McCarrick

- Archbishop Viganò said that he warned Pope Francis about McCarrick's corruption. But Pope Francis made the American prelate a trusted counselor.
- *Explanation*: At the time, McCarrick was charged with targeting seminarians who were legal adults. (Only recently have complaints involving minors emerged.) Pope Francis may not have thought that

homosexual activity with adult partners should disqualify a cleric from high office.

- Is that explanation consistent with the pope's track record? Yes.

In 2013, the pope appointed Msgr. Battista Ricca to a very sensitive post, making him prelate to the Vatican bank, the Institute for Religious Works (IOR), at a time when the IOR was under heavy criticism. When he was questioned about Msgr. Ricca's background, which included notorious homosexual escapades, the pope issued his famous rhetorical question: "Who am I to judge?" The pope drew a sharp distinction between consensual sexual activities—"They are not crimes, right?"—and sex with minors: "Crimes are something different; the abuse of minors is a crime."

Is it conceivable that the Vicar of Christ thought that a man who had seduced his seminarians should be freed from restrictions—and not only forgiven, but trusted as an adviser? That is the essence of Archbishop Viganò's testimony. Unfortunately, the available facts gave no reason to dismiss the charge.

Several ranking Vatican officials offered their own testimonies in support of Archbishop Viganò's claims. ("Viganò said the truth," was the simple comment from Msgr. Jean-Francois Lantheaume, who had worked with the former nuncio in Washington.)[15] In the United States, at least twenty bishops issued public statements saying that the charges contained in the archbishop's testimony should be thoroughly investigated. Only a few American prelates weighed in against the former diplomat, saying that his charges were divisive and unseemly. Without exception, these complaints came from bishops who had been criticized by name in the Viganò testimony: Cardinals Wuerl, Tobin, and Cupich and Bishop Robert McElroy of San Diego. Cardinal Cupich showed himself particularly tone-deaf about the controversy, telling a television interviewer that the pope should not go "down a rabbit hole" to investigate the scandal. In an inept statement that seemed to dismiss concerns about sexual abuse and Vatican corruption, Cardinal Cupich airily proclaimed, "The Pope has a bigger agenda."[16] He then cited the pope's concern about climate change.

Even before the release of the Pennsylvania grand-jury report and the Viganò testimony, the president of the US Conference of Catholic Bishops (USCCB), Cardinal Daniel DiNardo, had indicated that he would ask Pope Francis to authorize an apostolic visitation of the American hierarchy to investigate all aspects of the McCarrick scandal. An apostolic visitation (an investigation carried out with papal authorization) could require the cooperation of individual bishops and of Vatican bureaucrats—something that the bishops' conference could not do on its own authority. The request was an early indication that the American bishops were determined to unearth the facts.

Cardinal DiNardo made his request to Rome in mid-August. As the month came to an end, with the dual detonations from Pittsburgh and Viganò, he had not received a response. "I am eager for an audience with the Holy Father,"[17] the American cardinal said, betraying some impatience. At last the pontiff did agree, and on September 13, he met with a small delegation from the USCCB. After the meeting, Cardinal DiNardo reported a "lengthy, fruitful, and good exchange."[18] He said nothing about the prospects for an apostolic visitation.

But the situation had changed radically between the time when Cardinal DiNardo originally suggested a Vatican investigation and the time when he met with the Holy Father; the Viganò testimony had put an apostolic visitation in a very different light. A visitation, if conducted rigorously, could produce the documents that would prove conclusively whether or not Archbishop Viganò's testimony was accurate. It could identify the bishops, in the US and in Rome, who had helped to advance the ecclesiastical career of the disgraced ex-cardinal—and those whose careers McCarrick had advanced. It could expose the influence of the "lavender mafia" and the corruption of the Roman Curia. It could also give American Catholics at least some reason to believe that the Vatican was finally taking action, finally ending the years of cover-up.

In calling for an apostolic visitation, Cardinal DiNardo—with the apparent support of a majority of American bishops—was taking an extraordinary step. Knowing that the process would inevitably be painful, that ugly facts would emerge, that episcopal colleagues would be damaged, he nonetheless concluded that this dangerous operation was warranted to restore the battered credibility of the American hierarchy. The American bishops wanted the truth.

But did the pope? A week after their meeting with the pontiff, the leaders of the US bishops' conference announced a series of new actions: an independent investigation, led by lay experts; a new third-party reporting system for abuse;

a plan to hold bishops accountable for misconduct. Conspicuously missing from the list was an apostolic visitation. The pope, informed sources said—with more than a hint of annoyance—had turned down the request.

On the eve of his meeting with the USCCB delegation, Pope Francis made a grand gesture, announcing that he would call a meeting for representatives of all the world's episcopal conferences to "discuss the prevention of abuse of minors and vulnerable adults." That meeting was to take place in February 2019, more than five years after the pope had announced his plan for a special commission to devise policies for "the prevention of abuse of minors and vulnerable adults." One might ask: what had the commission been doing for those five years?

For one thing, the commission had been butting heads with various Vatican officials, trying—and often failing—to gain approval for its recommendations. Commission members had resigned in frustration, complaining about the lack of cooperation from other Vatican offices and episcopal conferences. If he saw the problem as urgent, the pope, as the Church's supreme legislator, could have *ordered* all episcopal conferences to adopt the commission's recommendations; he could have added those recommendations to the *Code of Canon Law.* Instead he was convening another meeting to discuss the topic.

Or rather, to discuss a *part* of the topic. The revelations of recent weeks had made it impossible to ignore two aspects of the scandal that had not been addressed: the influence of a homosexual network in the clergy and the complicity of bishops who had failed to address abuse complaints. Those problems were not mentioned in the Vatican's announce-ment for the worldwide summit meeting.

To be fair, the papal commission had recommended the creation of a special tribunal that would hold bishops accountable for their negligence in handling abuse charges. In 2015, the pontiff approved that recommendation and created the tribunal. On paper. But in reality nothing changed—it was all talk, again—and after a year, the pope announced another new policy, rescinding the plan for the tribunal, claiming that existing procedures were adequate for disciplinary handling of negligent bishops. Of course, if those procedures had worked effectively, the scandal of 2018 would not have occurred. So the pope was inviting the world's bishops to discuss a critical problem, ignoring the fact that to a large extent, the world's bishops *were* the problem.

Apart from grand plans for future discussion and bland promises of tough discipline, the pope offered no comments on the burgeoning scandal. After a September visit to the Baltic countries, the pope gave his usual in-flight press con-ference. But whereas in the past these exchanges with report-ers had often produced startling headlines, on this occasion reporters were grumbling about what the pope did *not* say; he did not answer questions about sexual abuse.

After fielding several questions about his time in the Bal-tics, the pope was asked by an Austrian reporter about a statement he had made in Estonia concerning Church pol-icies to curb sexual abuse. The pontiff said that he would not answer the question at that moment; he wanted more questions about his trip. But he did promise to address the issue later in the session.

Just one more question followed, about Lithuanian immigration. Then the papal spokesman, Greg Burke, acknowledged that there were no more questions about the trip. Rather than opening the floor for questions about the abuse issue, the pope addressed it himself in the course of a lengthy, rambling statement. After touching on other topics, he said that things are much better than they once were and the grand-jury report in Pennsylvania reflected "the way of thinking in previous times." He assured reporters that he had never offered leniency to a priest who was convicted of sexual abuse by the Congregation for the Doctrine of the Faith.

If the Holy Father had allowed questions on the topic, an enterprising reporter might have pressed him to speak about former cardinal Theodore McCarrick, whose name he had not mentioned. Or about Archbishop Viganò, whose name was also missing from the pope's remarks. Or Mauro Inzoli, an Italian priest who was removed from ministry by Pope Benedict XVI but restored by Pope Francis—temporarily, until new abuse charges forced his laicization. But the pope wasn't taking questions.

And reporters were not happy. A Twitter comment by Cindy Wooden conveyed the mood: "Shot down by Pope Francis. He only wanted questions on the trip to the Baltic countries. I said that I had questions left unanswered since returning from Dublin. They were trip questions. Just not this trip. #FoiledAgain #Vigano."

Cindy Wooden was not a troublemaker, not a gadfly, not a sensationalist. She was the Rome bureau chief for Catholic

News Service, the agency owned and operated by the US bishops' conference. If she was giving voice to her feelings, it was fair to assume that other reporters felt at least equally frustrated.

Thus far in his pontificate, Pope Francis has enjoyed remarkably favorable media coverage. He had not been pressed to answer awkward questions: about the *dubia*, about the dismantling of the Secretariat for the Economy, about declining morale in the Roman Curia, about Chile and McCarrick and Viganò and Wuerl and Pennsylvania and Germany. But now reporters were grumbling.

All through September the pope maintained his official silence about the abuse scandal, even while new reports of official corruption flashed around the world's media outlets. But while he made no public comment, and rarely mentioned the news stories, the pontiff gave a clear indication of his thinking in a series of angry homilies at weekday Masses. "With people who don't have good will, who seek only scandal, who want only division, who seek only destruction," he told a congregation on September 3, "silence and prayer" is the only appropriate response. He reminded the faithful that Jesus had not answered his accusers.

On September 11, the pope returned to the same theme, saying that the "Great Accuser"—Satan, presumably—was "attacking bishops" by providing damaging information "in order to scandalize the people." He continued to hammer home the same message all through the month, ending with a plea to the faithful to pray the Rosary daily during October, as a defense against the "Great Accuser" who was attacking the Church. It was not difficult for listeners to infer that the pope had particular scandal-mongers in mind, that he saw himself as the innocent victim of hateful attacks.

Finally, as September came to a close, one month after making his first damaging charges against Pope Francis, Archbishop Viganò ramped up the pressure on the pontiff with a second salvo. Perhaps equally important, he also began applying public pressure to other prelates, notably Cardinals Marc Ouellet and Daniel DiNardo.

"Neither the Pope, nor any of the cardinals in Rome have denied the facts I asserted in my testimony," Archbishop Viganò said. Then he challenged them to speak up.

To Cardinal DiNardo, the archbishop's challenge was simple and straightforward. He wanted the American prelates to announce to the world what insiders already knew: that Pope Francis had refused to authorize an apostolic visitation, thereby making it practically impossible to unearth all the facts surrounding the McCarrick scandal. Archbishop Viganò said that "the faithful deserve to know" what happened when the American bishops asked for an apostolic visitation. By announcing that fact to the world, rather than letting observers draw their own conclusions, Cardinal DiNardo would be joining Archbishop Viganò, not only in a public protest of the pontiff's policies, but in an open and sincere demand for transparency, honesty. If he were to do so, Cardinal DiNardo would be saying that God's people are entitled to the truth.

To Cardinal Ouellet, the prefect of the Congregation for Bishops, Archbishop Viganò issued a different sort of challenge. He praised the Canadian cardinal for having "maintained his dignity" at the start of the current pontificate but then said that Cardinal Ouellet "gave up" when he saw his work in the selection of bishops being undermined by members of the Vatican's lavender mafia. In other words, he was directly questioning Cardinal Ouellet's integrity. But he offered the cardinal a simple means of proving his good faith: "You have at your complete disposal key documents incriminating McCarrick and many in the Curia for their cover-ups. Your Eminence, I urge you to bear witness to the truth."

As a title for his second critical statement, Archbishop Viganò used the phrase that he had selected, years ago, as his episcopal motto: *Scio cui credidi*, "For I know whom I have believed" (2 Tm 1:12).

Chapter 3

The Divisions Revealed

Painful though they were, the ugly revelations about clerical abuse were not new stories in the summer of 2018, particularly for American Catholics. During the "long Lent" of 2002, when sensational headlines had appeared day after day, with new reports about predatory priests and negligent bishops, American Catholics had almost become accustomed to the scandal. Stories that might have merited front-page coverage in 2002 were now relegated to the back pages of newspapers: another priest convicted, another damaging diocesan memo exposed, another lawsuit settled—at a cost to the Church of tens of millions of dollars, to say nothing of the unspeakable harm that had been done to the victims.

Why was the McCarrick scandal different? Why was the anger among lay Catholics so much more virulent than it had been sixteen years earlier? Why did the revelations of the summer of 2018 shatter the already damaged credibility of the American hierarchy? There are several reasons:

1. McCarrick was by far the most prominent of the American prelates to be ousted because of sexual misconduct.

2. The bishops had never held themselves accountable for their behavior; they were immune from the disciplinary measures they imposed on ordinary priests.

3. McCarrick's misconduct had been flagrant, it had continued over a period of years, and within the ecclesiastical community, "everybody knew"—including Vatican officials.

4. McCarrick's case could not be classified as pedophilia. His preferences were clearly homosexual, and the description of his activities drew attention to the homosexual nature of most clerical abuse.

5. Bishops and other Church leaders who must have been aware of McCarrick's proclivities did not merely tolerate him. They actively promoted him. He continued to rise through the clerical ranks after his misconduct had been reported.

6. And so suspicions grew—and then Archbishop Viganò's testimony confirmed—that a powerful clique of homosexuals, a "lavender mafia," was active within the hierarchy, with its influence extending up to the Vatican.

The picture that emerged in the summer of 2018, then, was not simply a matter of sinful priests and overly lenient bishops. Something more sinister was visible here: a fifth column within the clergy, a cabal of priests (and bishops and even cardinals) with purposes radically at odds with the teachings of the Catholic Church.

When the scandals of 2018 are seen in that light, it is easy to explain why the secular media, which had been relentless in their coverage of sexual abuse during that "long Lent" of 2002, were far less interested in the latest revelations. McCarrick's fall from grace commanded headlines, and the Pennsylvania grand-jury report was analyzed in excruciating detail. The Viganò testimony and its implications, however, received only perfunctory coverage. Investigative reporters might easily have pursued any of the many leads that Archbishop Viganò had provided. But they did not. The mass media were not concerned with internal Catholic disputes. If anything, they were sympathetic to the cabal that was now under attack—or if not to McCarrick, at least to the former cardinal's allies.

The righteous anger of faithful Catholics was also largely ignored by the official Catholic media: those newspapers and broadcast outlets subsidized (directly or indirectly) by dioceses, dependent on the goodwill of the same bishops who were now the object of popular outrage. But a few independent Catholic publications and news services kept the story alive, with the powerful assistance of the online social media.

To pursue the story in more detail, let's return to those several respects in which the news of 2018 was more shocking to the lay faithful.

First, McCarrick was extremely prominent. Quite a few American Catholic bishops had resigned under pressure since 2002—either because they had blatantly ignored priestly misconduct or because they themselves were found guilty of abuse. But only one cardinal, the late Bernard Law, formerly of Boston, had resigned. And whereas Cardinal Law had failed to curb abuse by *other* priests, McCarrick himself was charged with abuse.

As cardinal-archbishop of Washington, DC, McCarrick had commanded nationwide attention. Indeed, he had served as a chief spokesman for the US bishops' conference in 2002, explaining the provisions of the Dallas Charter and blithely assuring television audiences that the American bishops were committed to wiping out clerical abuse. That *he* was now exposed as an abuser betrayed a stunning level of cynicism and hypocrisy.

Second, after promulgation of the Dallas Charter, the American bishops had confidently assured their people that they had the abuse problem firmly under control. Now it became clear that they did not. In 2002, the bishops frequently fell back on the excuse that in allowing predatory priests to return to parish assignments after short leaves of absence for evaluation and treatment, they were following the advice of trusted psychiatric professionals. (Why they trusted those particular professionals—and why they continued to trust them even when their advice had proven disastrous—is a question that was never addressed.) They had only recently come to understand the nature of pedophile behavior, the bishops said; Cardinal Law had spoken plaintively of a "learning curve." The emergence of new complaints, involving abuse that occurred after 2002, had slowed considerably; there were now dozens of new cases nationwide each year rather than hundreds. But those new cases were particularly egregious in light of the many reassurances that had been given.

Third, as the charges against McCarrick came to light, lay Catholics were reminded (in many cases, they learned for the first time) that the tough standards of the Dallas Charter did not apply to the bishops themselves. A parish priest could be removed from his assignment, and placed indefinitely in ecclesiastical limbo, if one complaint against him was deemed credible. But there was no provision for disciplinary action against a bishop. Even after two different dioceses had settled lawsuits brought by McCarrick's victims, "Uncle Ted" had remained in good standing.

Fourth, within days after news of McCarrick's suspension broke, dozens of informed Catholics had testified that they had been aware of the prelate's misdeeds for years. In other words, this was an open secret. Many knew and were silent. Rumors about the beach house on the New Jersey shore had circulated through the Catholic grapevine for decades. In 2002, a reporter for a major metropolitan newspaper told me to expect the "outing" of an American cardinal. I knew then that the reference was to McCarrick and fully expected the story to break. But that reporter, and apparently several others, could never find witnesses ready to testify for the record. Julia Duin, the longtime religion writer for the *Washington Times*, recalled that she had run into a wall of silence when she investigated the rumors. "There were priests and laity alike for whom McCarrick's predilections were an open secret," she said, "but no one wanted to go after him."[19]

For journalists, the reluctance to "go after" a prominent Catholic leader is understandable. No reporter wants to be accused of slandering a revered public figure, nor to be hit with a libel suit. Still, there had been plenty of hostile reports about Catholic bishops in the American media during the years between 2002 and 2018. Were reporters and editors also reluctant to tackle the McCarrick scandal because they preferred to maintain the standing of a liberal Catholic icon?

Still silence among journalists is not nearly as appalling as the complicity of other Church leaders. If "everybody knew," surely some American bishops knew. Why did they not confront McCarrick? Why did they not demand Vatican intervention? Why did they tolerate a predator?

Fifth, McCarrick's misconduct could not be classified as pedophilia. True, he was eventually removed from ministry because of a complaint lodged by a legal minor. But the misconduct for which he had become notorious did not involve children. His escapades at the beach house were arranged to seduce seminarians who were legal adults. He stepped across a crucial line, apparently, when he targeted a young man who was not yet a legal adult. His fellow bishops could say—accurately, if not altogether truthfully—that they were not aware McCarrick had abused minors. I was not aware, either, that he abused minors. Yet "everybody knew" that he abused seminarians who were under his authority.

Since the time of the Dallas Charter, spokesmen for the American bishops have taken great pains to insist that there is no scientific evidence of a tie between pedophilia and homosexuality. That statement is true, if the issue is "true" pedophilia—that is, an attraction to young children. The horrible cases of true pedophilia, involving the brutal molestation of children too young and innocent to understand what was happening to them, understandably caused the greatest outrage when the tales of abuse were told. But the vast majority of cases of sexual abuse involving Catholic clerics—well over 80 percent—involved teenage boys. An attraction to teenagers is not true pedophilia. McCarrick, with his groping of young men, was acting out a much more common homosexual impulse.

From the premise that homosexuality and pedophilia are not related, experts cited by the US bishops' conference have drawn the unwarranted conclusion that homosexual priests are no more likely than their heterosexual colleagues to engage in abusive behavior. Since the overwhelming preponderance of victims have been teenage boys, the illogic of that conclusion is illustrated neatly by the mordant observation of the late Father Richard Neuhaus: as between men who are sexually attracted to young men and men who are not sexually attracted to young men, the former are more likely to have sex with young men. In other words, the sex abuse crisis in the Catholic Church is rooted in homosexuality, not pedophilia, the protestations of too many bishops notwithstanding.

To bolster their claim that homosexuality is not a factor, some analysts have suggested that the number of female victims of sexual abuse might be under-reported. Perhaps so; we have no way of knowing how many young people were assaulted by clerics and, perhaps out of shame, never reported the incidents. But is it not likely that many young Catholic men, having been enticed into experimenting with homosexual activities, regretted their behavior and never told anyone about it? If only a fraction of abuse victims report the assaults, it is reasonable to conclude that many *more* male victims remain uncounted.

A sixth reason the new revelations have infuriated the Catholic laity to such a degree is that McCarrick not only survived in the ecclesiastical world but advanced through the ranks, even after his misconduct became commonly known. He was named Archbishop of Washington and given a cardinal's red hat after a delegation of prominent Catholics traveled to Rome to warn the Vatican against him. He served as a spokesman for the US bishops' conference—to discuss sexual abuse!—after reporters began asking questions about his beach house. He voted in a papal election after two different dioceses had been targeted by lawsuits involving his misconduct.

As Archbishop Viganò disclosed, McCarrick was finally reined in—however ineffectually—by Pope Benedict XVI. But then under Pope Francis, he returned to prominence as a papal emissary, taking on diplomatic missions to Cuba and China. He emerged as a papal confidant, promoting the ecclesiastical careers of other prelates; it was on his recommendation, apparently, that the pope conferred red hats on Cardinals Joseph Tobin and Blase Cupich. His own moral corruption—of which "everybody knew"—did not decrease his influence within the Catholic hierarchy. On the contrary, his prestige continued to grow.

And so finally, the McCarrick scandal heightened concern that a "lavender mafia" was active within the hierarchy, its powers reaching up into the Vatican. Archbishop Viganò's testimony confirmed the suspicions that McCarrick's prominence was attributable at least in part to the support of this homosexual clique and that he in turn supported the rise of other members. There was another, only slightly less cynical explanation for McCarrick's rise through the ecclesiastical ranks. From his earliest days he was known as a prodigiously successful fundraiser. As the key figure in the creation of the Papal Foundation, he was responsible for tens of millions of dollars that poured annually into the Vatican, to be disbursed for charitable projects. Cardinal Stanislaw Dziwicz—then Msgr. Dziwicz, private secretary to Pope John Paul II—reportedly pointed McCarrick out to a visitor as the future Archbishop of Washington, several months before the appointment was made.

Toward the end of his reign, a beleaguered Pope Benedict XVI—battered by the "Vatileaks" scandal in which dozens of confidential files had been leaked to the Italian media—formed an ad hoc commission of three retired cardinals—Julian Herranz, Salvatore De Georgi, and Jozef Tomko—to investigate the sex abuse scandal. All three cardinals on the commission were seasoned Vatican hands; all three were over the age of eighty. Pope Benedict appointed them, it seemed clear, because they would not be influenced by their own ecclesiastical ambitions, and they would not be participating in the next papal election. (Cardinals over eighty do not vote in a conclave.) The pontiff wanted an objective report.

In December 2012, the three cardinals delivered a massive dossier, reportedly running to over three hundred pages, which was prepared for the pope's eyes only. The contents of their report were never revealed. But the Vatican rumor-mill churned with stories that the cardinals had discovered a "lavender mafia" within the Roman Curia, and even named names.

When Pope Benedict resigned in February 2013, just a few weeks after the delivery of that secret report, and the world's cardinals gathered in Rome to choose his successor, the contents of the secret dossier became a matter of intense speculation. "The report is weighing on the conclave," Sandro Magister, a veteran Vatican journalist, told the *Wall Street Journal.* When Pope Francis was elected, and paid a courtesy call on his predecessor, news photos showed a thick file on the table between them. Evidently the retired pope handed the dossier over to his successor. And since that day, nothing more substantial about the cardinals' report—which might have been the basis for exposing the manifest corruption in the Roman Curia—has come to light.

According to Archbishop Viganò, Pope Francis has enjoyed the support of active homosexuals and their allies in the hierarchy and the pope has given them his support in turn. Could the suppression of the three cardinals' report be an instance of that cooperation? Here I am speculating, I readily admit. But the facts fit the hypothesis.

In fact, the Viganò testimony gave new life to all sorts of speculation. Conspiracy theories blossomed all across the internet. The summer of 2018 was not a good season for cautious Catholic journalists; the more radical Vatican-watchers drew far more attention. And that was only fair because the more radical theories of past years—involving cardinals with beach houses and bishops who covered up crimes and Vatican officials who suppressed investigations—were now being confirmed.

This much was clear, and had been clear for years: many bishops had withheld information about grievous clerical misconduct. In 2002, the public had learned about the bishops who transferred abusive priests from parish to parish. Now in 2018, we heard about bishops who said they had never heard about McCarrick's escapades. Cardinal Donald Wuerl, McCarrick's successor as Archbishop of Washington, said that he had never heard the stories that circulated all around his archdiocese. Cardinal Kevin Farrell, who had been vicar-general under McCarrick, and shared breakfast with him regularly, also professed complete ignorance. (In Cardinal Farrell's case, this was not the first instance of a remarkable ignorance; as a prominent member of the Legionaries of Christ, he had also said that he was unaware of the double life led by that movement's disgraced founder, Father Marcial Maciel.) How was it possible that these presumably intelligent men did not know what so many others around them knew? If they really were ignorant of the facts, were they extraordinarily obtuse? Or had they deliberately cultivated an ability to avoid a collision of inconvenient facts?

Earlier in 2018, before the McCarrick scandal erupted, the entire American hierarchy had been presented with an opportunity to demonstrate that learned ability to ignore evidence of a problem. In February, Cardinal Joseph Tobin of Newark (one of McCarrick's proteges), as he prepared for an airplane trip, sent off a cell-phone message which, although it was obviously a personal message, accidentally appeared on his public Twitter feed: "Supposed to be airborne in 10 minutes. Nighty-night, baby. I love you." Had Cardinal Tobin just unintentionally revealed something about himself? In answer to the obvious questions, a spokesman for the Newark archdiocese said that the message was intended for one of the cardinal's younger sisters.[20] And with that, the subject was closed; neither reporters nor anyone else pressed for more information. But in the cynical world of 2018, with the credibility of Catholic bishops irretrievably damaged, the subject could not, and should not, be closed. *Someone* should have asked follow-up questions.

We *know* that bishops have lied. We know that other bishops were aware of the lies. And we know that the liars have never acknowledged, much less apologized for, their offenses. The case-studies of 2002 had shown how often bishops, upon receiving a complaint about sexual abuse, had not only denied the truth but also attacked the messenger who brought the complaint.

Take just one admittedly egregious example. In October of 2003, some parishioners from a church in Merced, California wrote a letter to Fresno's Bishop John Steinbock complaining of the misconduct and heterodoxy of their pastor, Father Jean-Michael Lastiri. The principal signatory received this response from Bishop Steinbock:

> I support Fr. Michael Lastiri as pastor of St. Patrick's. He is a good and dedicated priest, faithful to the magisterium of the Church, living a chaste and faithful life of a good priest. The people of God at St. Patrick's have been blest by his presence and leadership. It is a grave sin against justice to state, "The members of our Parish have been so long without a chaste and faithful pastor . . ." This is defamation of character. Please refer

to the "Catechism of the Catholic Church" regarding this, paragraphs 2475 through 2479.

I certainly do not see in your letter the teaching and truth of Jesus Christ. I can only call you, and those who signed such a scandalous letter, to conversion to ask God's pardon and the pardon of your pastor whom you defame so maliciously. I will very much pray for all those who signed the letter, asking God to give them the grace to look within themselves to see how God may be calling them to conversion rather than simply judging and condemning others in generalities.[21]

Eight months after he wrote that letter, Bishop Steinbock removed the same Father Jean-Michael Lastiri from the parish after a lay organization called Roman Catholic Faithful posted screen-shots of Lastiri's internet solicitations to homosexuals. Later it emerged that Father Lastiri had misappropriated $60,000 in parish funds. Did the late Bishop Steinbock ever apologize to the faithful Catholics he had charged with scandal and defamation when they had reported the truth? No. Nor did other bishops apologize to the whistle-blowers whose warnings they had dismissed and whose integrity they had impeached. After the "long Lent," our bishops finally acknowledged that they had failed to rein in abusive priests. But they have never, to this day, admitted that they also failed to heed the warnings from the laity.

The warnings continue to this day, and still they are routinely ignored. If a priest violates the Dallas Charter, by initiating sexual contact with a legal minor, he will (if the bishop is minimally honest) be suspended from ministry. But if the priest is guilty of any other sort of misconduct—whether it is sexual activity with an adult, or preaching heresy, or indulging in liturgical abuse—a parishioner who complains can expect the same sort of reaction that victims of abuse encountered in the past: a flat denial of the problem, a claim that the person who complains is the guilty party, or perhaps, at best, an empty assurance that the problem will be addressed and he should stop worrying about it.

Today, in 2018, bishops are quick to assure their people that they have strict policies and iron-clad procedures for dealing with complaints of sexual abuse. In some cases, sadly, bishops have not adhered to their own policies, and the results have been disastrous.

But if lay Catholics felt that they could not trust their bishops, their skepticism was not rooted solely in concern about the sex-abuse scandal. For many years, American Catholics have become accustomed to thinking of their bishops as remote figures, distant from the everyday concerns of the faithful. Catholics who had other serious complaints—about liturgical abuses, perhaps, or even sacrilege—found that their complaints were stalled in chancery offices. To be sure, the *Code of Canon Law* included clear regulations to prevent such abuses and guaranteed the faithful the right to reverent liturgy. But the canons were enforced by the bishops, at the bishops' discretion. If the bishops choose not to take action—as was usually the case—the complaints had no effect.

Nor have American prelates been willing to enforce canon law in cases involving prominent political figures. In 2006, speaking to his brother bishops about proposals to deny the

Eucharist to politicians who supported abortion, none other than Cardinal Theodore McCarrick of Washington argued that such disciplinary action might close doors. It was much better, he pointedly remarked, to keep the doors open for cooperative work with politicians on issues such as funding for Catholic charities, Catholic schools, and Catholic hospitals. The cardinal—who said that he would not be "comfortable" withholding Communion—said that ecclesiastical discipline might give rise to the impression that the Church was meddling in partisan politics, and he noted that the late Cardinal Avery Dulles once remarked that "the Church incurs a danger of alienating judges, legislators and public administrators whose good will is needed for other good programs, such as the support of Catholic education and the care of the poor. For all these reasons, the Church is reluctant to discipline politicians in a public way, even when it is clear that their positions are morally indefensible."[22]

Notice that Cardinal McCarrick conceded that a pro-abortion Catholic politician's stand is "morally indefensible." In such a case, a stern rebuke would seem warranted, not only for the sake of public clarity, but also for the good of the politician's soul. But McCarrick put those considerations in second place, behind the considerations of how the public might perceive the disciplinary action.

How often does the fear of an angry public reaction deter Catholic bishops from doing or saying something that would promote the cause of faith? Certainly the American hierarchy has been reluctant to implement the clear instructions of canon law (Canon 915, specifically) that directs ministers to withhold the Eucharist from Catholics who "obstinately persist in manifest grave sin." The bishops have stated that support for unrestricted legal abortion is gravely sinful, and any reasonable person would agree that a politician's published remarks and recorded votes are surely a "manifest" indication of his persistence. But the American bishops, with a few honorable exceptions, have not yet drawn the obvious logical conclusion.

McCarrick cited the adverse political consequences that would be likely to follow upon any real disciplinary action against Catholic politicians who support the "culture of death." There would be angry editorials, certainly. Public sympathy might swing *toward* the wayward Catholic legislators so that, for political purposes, the disciplinary moves would seem counterproductive. But Catholic bishops should not allow political consequences to influence their pastoral decisions. Their duty is to keep the Church forthright and faithful in preaching the message of the Gospel—in this case, the Gospel of Life.

CHAPTER 4

The Habit of Denial

Have you ever noticed that when you recover from some minor illness—a common cold, perhaps, or a bout with the flu—you can never quite pinpoint the time when you are fully healthy again? After a few miserable days, you notice a trend in the right direction. You find yourself sniffling less frequently, sleeping more soundly, eating more regularly. You're tired of lazing on the couch and just ambitious enough to tackle your normal daily tasks. You go back to work. It's an effort; at the end of the day, you're exhausted. But the next day is a bit better.

Then a few days later, you wake up and go about your usual routine, forgetting that you've been sick until something reminds you and you realize: "I feel fine!" Your head is clear; your energy is back. You may not be an Olympic athlete, and you're definitely not as young as you used to be, but life is back to normal.

After years of tumult, life in the Catholic Church was nearly back to normal too, before the "Francis effect" renewed the turmoil that had prevailed for more than a generation. Or so it seemed. The acrimonious doctrinal debates, the grotesque liturgical abuses, the division of parishes into rival camps seemed to be receding into history.

For years, orthodox Catholics—"conservatives" if you like (although the political labels do not accurately convey the religious distinctions)—had sought out their own enclaves: stable parishes where they could be worship in peace, undisturbed by the novelties and absurdities that abounded in other churches. Any Sunday visit to another parish—on a vacation trip, perhaps, or a weekend in an unfamiliar city—brought a feeling of anxious dread. Would the priest improvise his own prayers, ignoring the text of the Missal? Would the music be deafening rock or bubble-gum pop? Would the homily be an exhortation for some left-wing political cause? Progressive or "liberal" Catholics flocked to their own favorite parishes, where pastors encouraged a skeptical attitude toward Roman pronouncements, guitarists strummed through the Eucharistic prayer, and bumper-stickers for Democratic Party candidates were prevalent in the parking lot.

To some extent, the fiery passions of the 1960s and 1970s had burned themselves out. The activists who had demanded radical changes in the Church eventually left, disappointed, or else retreated into their own separate camps. Priests who had led the liturgical rebellion deserted the priesthood; lay activists who had complained that the Mass was boring began to stay home on Sunday mornings, or find their own preferred liturgies on college campuses and chapels run by religious orders. The generation of Catholics who had been radicalized after Vatican II grew older and mellowed. The warring factions drew apart.

But the passage of time was not the only factor contributing to the gradual restoration of order in the Church. Years of clear papal teaching had an effect as well, gradually curtailing the excesses of post-conciliar experimentation. The *Catechism of the Catholic Church* provided an invaluable summary of what the Church actually teaches in a clear and readable form. A new translation of the Mass restored the dignity of the liturgical language and reined in priests who had developed a habit of freelancing their own Eucharistic prayers.

During the pontificate of Benedict XVI, one could sense a near-desperation among radical Catholics: the feeling that the long-awaited revolution within the Church had faltered and the window of opportunity was closing. To keep things in perspective, Pope Benedict also had his critics at the opposite end of the spectrum, issuing solemn warnings about schism and apostasy. And these conservative critics quickly burst into full voice when Pope Francis came to power, as the pope's public statements seemed to call into question the policies of his immediate predecessors. But until recently, those conservative critics represented only an infinitesimal fraction of the Catholic population. They were not a factor in the life of ordinary parishes.

The pendulum had swung, and now it is swinging back again. The Church finds stability somewhere near the center of the arc. There will always be disagreements and debates within the Church; that is entirely normal. But the community of the faithful is not ordinarily divided into warring camps. The past fifty years, through the era of post-conciliar confusion and contention, have been an aberration, an indication of grave problems that have not been resolved. Yes, they seemed to be receding, but then the unthinkable happened. Pope Benedict resigned. Surely a papal resignation, unless it is prompted by some debilitating health concern, is always a sign of trouble in the Church.

That said, viewed in light of history, it is not at all surprising that a major ecumenical council was followed by a generation of unrest. On the contrary, that has been the usual experience—one might almost say the "normal" experience—of the Church. Bishop James Conley of Lincoln, Nebraska, remarked on this phenomenon in a column he wrote for his diocesan newspaper:

> Historically, Church councils, like Vatican II, always bring some measure of confusion to the Church's life. Blessed John Henry Cardinal Newman once wrote that Church councils "always savor of the soil from which they sprang." In the case of Vatican II, the soil was the "sixties." In the post-conciliar period, the good fruit of the Council was intermingled, regrettably, with the anti-nomianism, anti-authoritarian, "free-love" spirit of the zeitgeist. There was confusion even among the theologians of the Vatican.
>
> Newman reflected that one must get a bit downstream from a council—fifty, seventy-five, one-hundred years—before the water clarifies and the stream gains strength and force.[23]

If Cardinal Newman was right (and he usually was), we

are roughly on schedule. Fifty years after the opening Vatican II, we were beginning to understand the true message of the council. That message is very different from the ballyhooed "spirit of Vatican II" that has been invoked so often in support of radical initiatives. Still, the council did have a powerful message, calling for changes within the Church. After a generation of separating the wheat from the chaff, the essential from the inessential, the Catholic world was coming to grips with the council's teachings.

One reason for the confusion that arose after Vatican II may be the fact that most Catholics did not perceive the need for such an ecumenical gathering. A council, ordinarily, is summoned to confront a crisis in the life of the Church. Thus, the Council of Chalcedon was convened to settle heated disputes on Christology, the Council of Trent to answer the challenge of the Reformation. But in the 1960s, most Catholics—at least certainly most American Catholics—thought the Church was quite healthy. Everything seemed to be going so well! The parish churches were full, the parochial schools were churning out graduates, vocations to the priesthood and religious life were at all-time highs. Nevertheless, St. John XXIII saw trouble ahead. He recognized the need for *aggiornamento*: a modernization, not of doctrine, but of attitude.

George Weigel, in his provocative book *Evangelical Catholicism*, advances the theory that Vatican II was a watershed event in a long historical development that began with Pope Leo XIII in the last years of the nineteenth century. Since the Council of Trent in the 1500s, Weigel argues, the leadership of the Catholic Church had been guided by the vision of that council, which gave rise to the Counter-Reformation, responding to the rise of Protestantism by emphasizing doctrinal orthodoxy and personal piety. That strategy produced enormous gains for Catholicism over the centuries. But as the times changed, so did the pastoral challenges facing the Church. By the twentieth century, the greatest threat to the faith came not from Protestants who rejected key tenets of Catholic doctrine but from secular ideologies that rejected Christianity as a whole. The mission of the Church was no longer to guard against erroneous interpretations of the Gospel but to persuade the world that the Gospel is worth reading.

In the sixteenth century, Catholics could safely assume that their neighbors, if not themselves Catholics, were at least Christians and respectful of the basic ideas of Christian civilization. Not so in the troubled twentieth century, nor in these early years of the twenty-first. Now we are faced with the same task that faced the earliest disciples of Jesus Christ: to go out into the world and make converts from among the skeptics and the enemies of faith. When he summoned the Second Vatican Council, St. John XXIII probably did not anticipate the tsunami of secularization that would engulf the West in the next generation, forcing future pontiffs to speak about "reconversion." But he did, with the guidance of the Holy Spirit, foresee the need for a new form of evangelization, a new strategy for bringing the Word of God to the modern world.

To restore the missionary zeal that fired the early Christians, the fathers of Vatican II called for a *ressourcement*: a return to primary sources, to the wellsprings of fundamental

Christian thought. Far from promoting a revolution in the Church, the council urged a back-to-basics approach. Yes, the council called for a radical change in orientation—but on the part of secular society, not the Church. Read the documents of Vatican II and the theme that emerges clearly is the need for the Church to transform society, certainly not to be transformed *by* the secular world.

If Pope John XXIII saw that need when he called for the council, his successors on the Throne of Peter treated it as a matter of steadily increasing urgency. St. John Paul II set a new model for the papacy, flying around the world to bring his message directly to the people. Both John Paul II and Benedict XVI spoke frequently about the "new evangelization," the quest to revive the Faith in societies where it had withered. Both pontiffs produced profound encyclicals and exhortations, clarifying fine points of doctrine. But they balanced those documents with constant reminders that, in its essence, the Christian faith is directed not toward a body of thought but toward a Person, Jesus Christ.

St. John Paul II urged the world, again and again, to look upon the face of Christ. Following his lead, Pope Benedict XVI set aside time during his pontificate to write a three-volume work, *Jesus of Nazareth*, to re-introduce readers to the person of Christ. Now Pope Francis encourages Christians to see Christ in others, and particularly those in need. There is a natural continuity in the way these three pontiffs sought, from different perspectives, to focus attention on Jesus, leading the Christian world back to the most fundamental basis of the Faith.

When he appeared on the loggia of St. Peter's basilica as

the newly elected pope on October 16, 1978, John Paul II wasted no time in delivering a call for spiritual renewal. "Be not afraid!" he told the audience in St. Peter's Square. "Open up—no, swing wide—the gates to Christ." Pope Benedict XVI offered a strikingly similar message in the homily during the Mass that formally inaugurated his ministry: "Do not be afraid of Christ! He takes nothing away, and he gives you everything." At his installation Mass, however, Benedict added an ominous note, asking the faithful, "Pray for me, that I may not flee for fear of the wolves."

Meanwhile, closer to home, the Church in the United States had seen its own institutional changes in the past generation. The activist bishops of the 1970s had retired. A new generation of prelates, heavily influenced by John Paul II, had come to the fore in the episcopal conference. For the Church in America, as for the universal Church, the time was ripe for structural reform.

To have been successful, however, that reform needed to eliminate habits that had taken deep root within the clerical culture. One such habit, regrettably quite common in the institutional Church, was and still is the tendency to ignore problems, to dodge responsibility, to pass the buck. Pastors, including bishops, had, over time, developed a penchant for the see-no-evil approach. If they could pretend that a problem did not exist, then they could make excuses for their failure to address that problem: their failure to exercise genuine spiritual leadership. Tragically, those bad habits of the episcopate and clergy were not eliminated.

An analogy is in order here. What would you think of a father who, when he saw signs that his children were headed for trouble, scurried to ensure that *he* would not be blamed? Suppose he noticed that his teenage son was regularly coming home at night with alcohol on his breath, and he reacted by writing a neat little essay for the local newspaper about the perils of underage drinking. Would you say that father had discharged his parental duties? Would you say that he had shown his love for his own? Of course not!

Pastors, too, have parental duties. A priest acts toward his people as a spiritual father. (Catholics give priests the title "Father" in recognition of that special relationship.) The pastor's task is to care for souls, not to preserve appearances. But in the Church today, the desire to maintain appearances without taking effective action—seeking only what might be described as a sort of ritual purity—too often impels clerics to ignore signs of trouble, to turn a blind eye to obvious difficulties, to sweep problems under rugs, in order to avoid unpleasantness and maintain an untroubled façade.

Think how often a pastor is tempted to gloss over a difficulty, to overlook signs of trouble. When children in a religious-education class fail to answer even the most basic questions about the Faith, he can chalk up their silence to reticence rather than ignorance and give them all passing grades. (When a Catholic Press Association survey asked Catholics aged fifteen to seventeen to name the four Gospels, only 37 percent could do so, and 56 percent could not name even one; 24 percent could not explain why Christians celebrate Easter.) If a young couple comes to his office for marriage preparation and each lists the same home address on the required form, he can blithely *assume* that they have separate apartments, or at least separate bedrooms. (If he makes an issue of their living arrangements, he knows full well that they are likely to walk out on him and find another priest who is more accommodating.) If a young curate is spotted emerging from a gay bar, he can *hope* that there is an innocent explanation. In each of these hypothetical cases, the pastor who says nothing is shirking his responsibilities. Yet he is leaving no "paper trail" of his negligence. He can at least pretend that he did not notice the problem and so maintain his ritual purity.

This desire for "ritual purity" is, if anything, more pronounced at the upper levels of the Catholic hierarchy, and most visible of all at the Vatican. Take the dramatic case of Msgr. Nunzio Scarano, who gained notoriety in 2013 when he was arrested and charged with attempting to bring €26 million into Italy illegally. Msgr. Scarano, who had been director of accounting at the Vatican's financial office, the Administration of the Patrimony of the Apostolic See, was already under investigation on money-laundering charges. As the prosecution explained the case against him, the world learned that Msgr. Scarano had extensive financial ties to powerful Italian business magnates, that he was known as "Msgr. €500" because of his penchant for flashing wads of high-denomination bills, and that he owned a luxurious apartment lined with expensive artwork. "We asked ourselves, how did this monsignor come to own this place and possess these expensive works of art," an investigator told the Reuters news service.[24] It was a natural question to ask. But somehow Msgr. Scarano's supervisors at the Vatican had failed to ask it. A priest who was flaunting his own personal wealth remained in his Vatican office—handling financial affairs, no less!—until public prosecutors intervened. How could a minor prelate have built up a financial empire while working for the Church, and done it all without prompting his superiors to investigate?

Two common human traits strengthen the tendency to avoid problems. One is the normal desire to avoid unpleasant confrontations. The role of a pastor is to unite, not to divide, and most priests are not aggressive personalities. The other, closely related factor is the willingness to give everyone the benefit of the doubt. In combination, unfortunately, these two characteristics—healthy and even laudable in themselves—can produce a sort of cockeyed optimism or willful blindness, a stubborn refusal to recognize reality. We *want* to see virtue in others, and sometimes we can only see it if our eyes are shut tight.

For the sovereign pontiff, pastor for the universal Church, there is another consideration that weighs against stern disciplinary measures. The duty of the Roman pontiff is to preserve unity among the faithful. If he cracks down on abuses—any sort of abuses—the pope, any pope, might risk dividing his flock. If he demands that recalcitrant priests and theologians end their dissent from formal Church teaching, they may choose instead to leave the Church, bringing their followers with them. Rather than risk schism, the pope may choose to accept an uneasy truce between Catholic factions that seem irreconcilable. This, it seems clear, was the path chosen by John Paul II and Benedict XVI.

If Church leaders are prone to overlooking current problems, they are equally likely to downplay past failures. Despite the grave losses that Catholicism has suffered during the past fifty years—the thousands who have left the Church, the families that have broken apart, the priests and religious who have forsaken their vows, the parishes and schools that have been closed—bishops remain reluctant to calculate the total damages and identify the root causes of the disaster.

In the years following Vatican II, thousands of priests walked away from their duties to begin a new life in the secular world. When they left, there was no formal announcement. The rumor mills buzzed, but there was no explanation of their departure. They simply disappeared; their names were removed from the diocesan directories. Wouldn't a healthier institution have been more forthright, admitting that these young priests had deserted their ministry? It might have been useful to suggest that they needed prayers; it would have been understandable, if not charitable, to denounce them. Instead there was only silence. Particularly for those who have embraced a false optimism or willful blindness, it seems pointless to dwell on painful memories. Far better to speak confidently about the future!

But reforms can succeed only if the real problems have been identified. Successful leadership requires a recognition that some decisions were unwise, some officials were misguided, some initiatives were destructive. Some of the programs enthusiastically embraced by Church leaders in the 1960s and 1970s led the faithful astray; we should try to understand what went wrong and try to help those who have been harmed.

Or to put it differently, any competent business executive looking at a corporate chart that showed a steady decline in profits over the course of years would recognize that the corporation had been doing something wrong, something that must be stopped. The hierarchy of the Catholic Church never showed the same basic understanding.

In the world of espionage, when a spy is revealed to be a double agent working for the enemy, his supervisors move quickly to assess the damage, to see what secrets he might have betrayed and what false information he might have delivered. The Church is not an espionage agency, of course, and only a fool would suggest that bishops behave like counter-intelligence operatives. Still, it would be prudent to ask questions about the motivations of some would-be reformers.

For example, if the founder of a movement within the Church later renounces the Faith, would it not be reasonable to ask whether the movement has been infected by the weaknesses and errors that prompted his apostasy? If the director of a parish religious-education office announces that she plans to be ordained as a female priest, is it unnatural to wonder whether she has been giving students an accurate understanding of Church teaching on the nature of the priesthood?

Similar questions could be asked about hundreds of people who are still employed in parish and diocesan ministry or teaching in Catholic schools. A conscientious pastor should satisfy himself that instructors in religious-education programs are teaching authentic Catholic doctrine. He might take special care with employees who were recruited through advertisements in the *National Catholic Reporter.* Since 1968, that independent weekly newspaper has been operating in defiance of the local bishop, who instructed the editors to remove the word *Catholic* from the title of the publication.

If loyal readers of the *National Catholic Reporter* are teaching our children's catechism classes, and conveying the ideas found regularly in that paper's editorial columns, then they are depriving those children of their heritage, withholding from them the truths of the Faith.

Moreover, those purveyors of dissent are endangering their own spiritual welfare. In *The Devastated Vineyard*, Dietrich von Hildebrand wrote with sorrow about the cleric who loses his faith. Then he added, "But it is much worse when, although he has lost the true faith, he remains within the Church and poisons the faithful through his influence. This is worse for him, too, he adds to the awful sin of heresy that of lying, deceiving others, abusing his dignity as a Catholic, and, in the case of a priest, abusing the trust which he possesses as a spokesman for the Church."

One of the great untold stories of the post-conciliar era involves the many influential theologians, liturgists, church musicians, and religious educators who have quietly left the Church. Had they already strayed from orthodoxy even as they were serving in the Church, shaping the faith of many young Catholics? If so, how much damage did they do before they left? Astonishing as it seems, more than a few ex-priests and ex-nuns have stayed on as teachers in religious education programs even after renouncing their vocations. Have some of them used their influence to pass on their own complaints against the Church? To ask these questions is not to call for a witch hunt but to recognize the need for careful discernment of spirits, one of the proper duties of Catholic bishops.

An honest appraisal of the past fifty years should brace us

for the conclusion that there are many diocesan programs that should never have been launched, liturgical innovations that should never have been suggested, hymns that should never have been sung. There are also priests who should not have been ordained, religious who should never have taken vows, and couples who should never have married. In *Will Many Be Saved*, the theologian and evangelist Ralph Martin remarks that at a time of obvious collapse in Catholic belief and Catholic morality, it may be necessary for some people to submit anew to the rites of baptism or marriage since they were not sincere in their original approach to the sacraments. Without impugning the validity of any individual's baptism, or any couple's marriage, a pastor might encourage his parishioners to examine their own consciences and come forward if they recognize the need to remedy a serious problem in the past.

But there has never *been* an honest effort by the hierarchy to make an accounting of what has happened to the Church in the past fifty years. Instead there has been a concerted effort to ignore the evidence of a spectacular pastoral failure. Mass attendance has plummeted; tens of thousands of priests and religious have abandoned their vocations; the Eucharistic liturgy has become a source of division rather than unity; religious education has been "dumbed down" to the point that few young Catholics can name the Ten Commandments or the seven sacraments; lapsed Catholics now represent the fastest-growing religious cohort in the United States. Still, Church leaders speak of "vibrant" communities, placidly ignoring the overwhelming evidence of an unmitigated disaster.

To some extent, the disaster was masked by the orthodox papacies of John Paul II and Benedict XVI. Faithful Catholics could point with pride to the teachings of those two pontiffs and believe—as they devoutly wanted to believe— that help was on the way. Timid bishops could endorse the statements issuing from the Vatican while doing little or nothing to put those statements into practice. At the parish level, however, the papal preaching had little effect. The banal liturgies, the vapid religious-education programs, and the heterodox theological programs all continued, as did the massive exodus of young Catholics from the Church. One could paraphrase the old adage about Nero and observe that it seems too many bishops have fiddled while Rome burns.

Nowhere has the breakdown in Catholic unity been more evident than in the field of morality, specifically, sexual morality. In 1968, the encyclical *Humanae Vitae* by Pope Paul VI affirming the traditional condemnation of artificial contraception was met with open resistance by Catholic theologians, and the hierarchy chose not to discipline the dissenters. Since that time, dissent has become commonplace not only on the question of contraception but on homosexuality, same-sex marriage, divorce, and abortion. In 1926, the great Catholic apologist G. K. Chesterton predicted, "The next great heresy is going to be simply an attack on morality; and especially on sexual morality." He was right.

Priests told Catholic couples that they should make their own decisions about using contraception, and their bishops remained silent. Theologians testified at legislative sessions in favor of same-sex marriage, and their bishops were silent. Diocesan tribunals routinely granted annulments to couples who had been married for decades and had several children, and their bishops remained silent. The bishops issued public statements upholding the formal teachings of the Church but took no action when those teachings were violated. The public dissent and the problems were obvious to all, as was the failure of Church leaders to respond.

In a typical American Catholic parish today, only a small handful of people take advantage of the opportunity for sacramental confession on Saturday (if the parish even offers that sacrament on a regular basis), but hundreds line up to receive Communion on Sunday. One would have to be willfully blind or childishly optimistic to deny that simple arithmetic supports the conclusion that many Catholics are receiving the Eucharist while in a state of sin, committing sacrilege and endangering their immortal souls. But priests do not preach about sacrilege. In the same ordinary parish, if the public-opinion surveys are right (and there is no real reason to doubt them), 90 percent of married couples of childbearing age are using artificial contraceptives in defiance of Church teaching. But priests do not preach about contraception. At diocesan marriage tribunals, the vast majority of couples seeking annulments receive them. If those tribunals are judging honestly, then thousands of Catholics have entered into invalid marriages. But priests typically do not preach about the requirements for a valid marriage.

Oh, a few priests do preach on these hot-button issues. But they are regarded as troublemakers, the exceptions to the rule of business as usual. Why should a pastor demand that cohabiting couples separate before their marriage if another pastor just down the road will make no such demand? Why should he refuse to administer the Eucharist to couples who have divorced and entered into a new civil marriage when they are welcomed for Communion at the neighboring parishes? Why should a young priest court unpopularity—and in all likelihood lose any chance he might have of becoming a bishop—by swimming against the current? Of course, there is an answer to that "why" question, and it is provided by the God made man who founded the Church, Jesus Christ, who came to bring not peace but the sword and who asked his own probing questions: "For what does it profit a man, to gain the whole world and forfeit his life?" (Mk 8:36).

For those priests who do become bishops, the years of training in rosy optimism have their effect. A bishop who hears that one of his priests is preaching heresy assumes that the report is exaggerated, that the appalled layman who makes the complaint is guilty of some misunderstanding or is some type of scrupulous fanatic. When a young priest is spotted in tight leather pants emerging from a gay bar, the bishop assumes that he entered the bar by mistake. He has years of practice in assuming the best; he is almost constitutionally incapable of imagining the worst—even when the worst is far more likely. Or perhaps, still worse, the bishop is fully cognizant of what the evidence suggests and chooses to hide behind the pretense of ignorance, to avoid a confrontation that might disrupt his ecclesiastical career, or at least his comfort.

This is the attitude, the training, the force of habit that played into the scandal of sexual abuse. When a priest was caught *in flagrante* with an altar boy, or when parents brought solid evidence of misconduct, the bishop could fall back on his placid assumption that there *might* be some innocent explanation, or that this *might* have been an isolated incident, or that the priest *might* respond to psychological treatment, and in the long run all will be well, as long as the offenses are kept quiet.

For a different sort of evidence of failure to confront a glaring problem, consider the statement issued early in 2014 by Archbishop José Rodriguez Carballo, the secretary of the Congregation for Religious, saying that religious communities worldwide are "really enjoying good health at this moment."[25] The same archbishop had previously disclosed that each year, about three thousand consecrated religious drop out of their communities. How could that daunting statistic be reconciled with a report of "good health" in religious life?

Archbishop Rodriguez Carballo explained his claim by saying, "There is a lot of holiness in our monasteries." No doubt there are many monks and nuns leading exemplary lives. But do their good examples justify an overall verdict that religious life is healthy? Which sort of religious community predominates numerically in the Church today: the vigorous, growing religious orders or those that are dying out for want of new vocations? With his pious report that one can find holiness in monasteries, the archbishop ducks that crucial question. We should expect more candid, hardheaded analysis from an official whose office is responsible for appraising the health of religious life. And in the same interview in which he spoke of "good health" in religious life, Archbishop Rodriguez Carballo let an inconvenient truth slip out. "There is a lot more holiness than what there

THE HABIT OF DENIAL

often appears to be," he said. He acknowledged, then, that there "often appears to be" a serious problem with contemporary religious life.

In the United States, that problem is manifest in the Leadership Conference of Women Religious (LCWR), the umbrella group that represents scores of women's religious orders. In 2008, at a conference on religious life, Cardinal Franc Rodé—who at the time was prefect of the Congregation for Religious—pointed out that many of these women's orders were disappearing, as current members grew old and died and few young women joined. (The more conservative religious orders, which were not affiliated with the LCWR, were far more successful in recruiting young members.) Cardinal Rodé said that the dying religious orders fell into two categories: those that "accept the present situation of decline" and those that "have opted for ways that take them outside communion with Christ in the Catholic Church, although they have opted to stay in the Church physically."[26]

Was Cardinal Rodé exaggerating? Just the previous year, the keynote speaker at an LCWR convention, Dominican Sister Laurie Brink, announced openly that some communities of women religious had "grown beyond the bounds of institutional religion." She asked rhetorically, "Who's to say that the movement beyond Christ is not, in reality, a movement into the heart of God?"[27] Such radical statements led the Vatican, after an investigation of the group, to announce in April 2012, "The current doctrinal and pastoral situation of LCWR is grave and a matter of serious concern." The Vatican ordered a program of reform, and in May 2013, Pope Francis signaled his determination to carry out that reform, reeling the LCWR back into the realm of Catholic orthodoxy. The pope remarked, "It is an absurd dichotomy to think of living with Jesus but without the Church, or following Jesus outside the Church, or loving Jesus without loving the Church."[28]

So the reform of the LCWR was underway. But in April 2015, the process ground to a halt with a Vatican statement that the LCWR is "fostering a vision of religious life that is centered on the Person of Jesus Christ and is rooted in the Tradition of the Church." The movement for reform was over. Sister Sharon Holland, the president of the LCWR, reported of her group's talks with the Vatican leadership: "We learned that what we hold in common is much greater than any of our differences."[29] At first glance, those two statements seem unremarkable, even banal. On closer inspection, however, they illustrate the depth of the tension between the LCWR and the hierarchy. Shouldn't it go without saying that the lives of Catholic religious communities would be centered on Christ and that the leaders of those communities would hold basic doctrinal beliefs in common with Vatican officials? Yet these affirmations—which would seem to indicate a rock-bottom minimum of shared faith—were deemed sufficient to explain why the Vatican chose to end the movement for reform.

Oddly enough, while American bishops have been extraordinarily patient with proponents of theological dissent and liturgical novelty, they have often been quite intolerant of criticism from the other end of the spectrum. "It is especially infuriating," wrote Dietrich von Hildebrand, "when certain bishops, who themselves show lethargy toward heretics, assume a rigorously authoritarian attitude toward those believers who are fighting for orthodoxy, who are thus doing what the bishops ought to be doing themselves."

Which Catholics are criticized more frequently in diocesan newspaper editorials: those who persistently attack the Church's teachings on controversial issues or those who stalwartly defend them? Sadly, the latter. Catholic groups lobbying for the ordination of women are treated more cordially than those asking for the widespread availability of the traditional Latin Mass. Bishops are more likely to rebuke loyal Catholics who complain about religious-education programs than to correct the teachers who are introducing strange ideas. Pious Catholics learn, to their sorrow, that often Church leaders are more polite to those who have contempt for doctrine than they are to those who strive to live their lives in accordance with it.

Why is this? One main reason, it seems, is that our bishops learned from experience that they can use their authority to rein in critics on one end of the spectrum but not the other. Dissident Catholics who reject the authority of the hierarchy will not respond well when a bishop lays down the law. Quite the contrary, they will cite the bishop's disciplinary action as further evidence of the "patriarchal" attitudes they are seeking to change. Catholics who respect the bishop's authority may grumble about his policies, but ultimately they will feel bound in conscience to accept them. A lukewarm Catholic who attends Mass only occasionally may stop practicing altogether if his parish introduces changes that he finds uncongenial. But a pious Catholic, feeling the force of his moral obligation to attend Sunday Mass, will keep coming, however unhappily.

In short, the rules are applied to those who will obey the rules. Years ago I spoke at some length to a priest who headed the "Office of Worship" in a major American archdiocese. He complained that his office was swamped with complaints from "conservative" Catholics—who he believed (rightly) were my friends and allies. Why were they so petty, he asked me; why were they so obsessed with the rules? I explained that the "rules" were the only defense that loyal Catholics had against liturgists who felt themselves at liberty to change any aspect of the Mass on impulse.

The "rules" of the liturgy are a guarantee that faithful Catholics will experience the Mass as the universal Church intends. The "rules" of defined doctrine are a guarantee that the content of the faith will be passed down in pure, unadulterated form. The "rules" of canon law are a guarantee that the rights of the faithful will be vindicated. But those rules are no guarantee at all if they are not enforced, or enforced selectively.

Dissident Catholics have been able to parlay the double standard into a virtual immunity from disciplinary action. As long as they can maintain their own sort of ritual purity, avoiding any clear and direct conflict with Church teachings, they can be confident that their ecclesiastical superiors will not take action. So liberal theologians rarely say, in so many words, that they disagree with Church teachings on sexual morality; instead they question whether those teachings should be given greater nuance. "Respectable" Catholic feminists—that is, those who remain within the orbit of official Catholicism—do not issue forthright calls for the ordination of women; they merely say that discussion of the question should not be suppressed.

For a quarter-century, the leaders of American Catholic colleges and universities have been engaged in an unproductive dialogue with the bishops over the implementation of *Ex Corde Ecclesiae*, the papal directive that, if enforced, would ensure a Catholic institution of higher education maintained a distinctively Catholic identity. Commenting on those long-running discussions in 2013, an anonymous Georgetown law professor told the Reuters news service, "There is a dance that has to be done with the Church and the students."[30] Agile dancers they, those forming minds and hearts at the largest Catholic universities which proudly advertise themselves as Catholic institutions, yet do not submit to the standards that the Church has set.

For decades, the hierarchy has strained to cope with the deep divisions among the Catholic faithful, without ever acknowledging them. Radical differences in faith have been treated as problems to be managed rather than challenges to be resolved. Thus, our hierarchy, by failing to grapple with serious problems, has allowed the development of two opposing camps among the Catholic faithful.

Pope Pius XI once called in a prominent American Jesuit diplomat to brief him on the anti-Catholic persecutions of the day: the atheistic Soviet regime that was sending Russian believers to the gulags; the Mexican government that was hunting down priests and executing them; the anti-clerical campaign in Spain that would produce such pathological hatred during that country's civil war. The pope listened reflectively to the priest's report, then posed a rhetorical question: "Tell me, Father Walsh, who have been the worst persecutors of the Church?" After a pause, Pope Pius answered his own question: "The Church's worst persecutors have been her own unfaithful bishops, priests, and religious. Opposition from the outside is terrible; it gives us many martyrs. But the Church's worst enemies are her own traitors."

Our bishops, the successors to the Apostles, have a responsibility as shepherds to guard their flocks against dangers, including those particularly insidious dangers that arise from within the Church. By ignoring the obvious dangers that have troubled the Catholic world for decades—and worse, suppressing the complaints of honest lay Catholics who reported on those dangers—the bishops have failed in their duties and betrayed their people.

In the military world, no effective force ever tolerates traitors, deserters, or informers. Today, in the midst of our "culture wars," the Catholic Church can ill afford to wage a two-front battle: against militant secularists on one hand and renegade Catholics on the other. The first order of business for anyone serious about Church reform should be to restore unity within the ranks.

CHAPTER 5

With Apologies to the Martyrs

In the mid-seventeenth century, the leading cause of death among the Jesuits working in North America was martyrdom.

What was it that compelled bright young men from comfortable French families to travel to an unknown and uncivilized country, to live in squalor, to suffer hunger and deprivation and disease? Why did they keep coming, and keep preaching, even when they realized that they faced not merely a risk but a certainty of violent death? Why did St. Isaac Jogues, after he was tortured by the Iroquois, escape to France, where he was hailed as a living martyr—and then, giving up that life of honor and comfort, seek permission to go back to the Iroquois territory, where he knew that he would be killed?

Those intrepid missionaries wanted to preach the Gospel. They wanted to save souls. They believed—and acted boldly on the belief—that the opportunity to bring people to Christ was more valuable than their own lives. They also believed—and told the native Americans to whom they preached—that salvation could come only through faith in Jesus Christ and incorporation into the Catholic Church. And their belief in the necessity for redemption sprang from the belief that unredeemed men were in danger of eternal damnation: a belief that they conveyed in their preaching.

How many Catholics—indeed, how many Catholic missionaries—hold those same beliefs today? How many would be willing to proclaim those beliefs to an unfamiliar and quite likely hostile audience? How many truly believe that the opportunity to convey the Gospel message is worth the risk of offending an audience, worth the risk of being rejected and scorned, worth even the risk of life itself? If the work of evangelization is not worth those risks, then why do we honor the martyrs who took them? Were they foolish? Were they intemperate zealots motivated by noble ideals, no doubt, but wanting in prudence? Did they, in the end, do any good for those pagan tribes?

Those seventeenth-century Jesuits were not bringing economic assistance to the American natives. They had nothing to give—nothing material, that is. Although most of them came from reasonably affluent families, they did not come to America to engage in what we might now term "charitable work." Still less were they interested in social engineering to raise the standard of living among the Indian tribes. If they taught some natives to read, and treated some who were sick, those were secondary activities. Their overarching purpose was to spread the Catholic faith.

Today we honor the Jesuit missionaries as saints. Yet many Catholic Americans place no particular importance on the goal that motivated those martyrs: the salvation of souls. On the contrary, many twenty-first-century Christians criticize the early Jesuit missionaries for imposing their European moral standards on an indigenous culture. Others, slightly more generous toward the missionaries, would suggest that they would have served the Indians better by helping them raise their standards of living without worrying so much about the state of their souls.

For Isaac Jogues and Jean de Brebeuf and René Goupil and Jean de Lalande and others like them, it was a matter of the utmost urgency to tell the Native Americans about Jesus Christ. That urgency is sadly missing from the Catholic Church today in the land where the Jesuits' blood was shed. Even Church organizations dedicated to the missions hesitate to say that bringing people into the Catholic faith is their top priority. In 1995, the executive director of the US Catholic Mission Association, Lou McNeil, told the *New York Times*, "There's a greater sense that all religions have value, and there's no compelling reason why we need to change people's religion."

Were those Jesuit martyrs foolish, then, to throw away their lives on an unnecessary mission? Or do we think that we have become so sophisticated that we can see elements of Christianity in any set of beliefs, and even in unbelief? *Something* is wrong here. Either we are wrong to revere the martyrs, since they were wrong to sacrifice themselves, or else we are wrong to shrink from the bold proclamations of faith that they made.

One wonders what kind of homilies those young men heard in their formative years. What words from their own bishops and priests so touched their hearts and fired them with zeal for the Gospel that they would go to distant lands to be martyred for the cause of Christ? Do our young men and women hear such words from the pulpit today? If not, why not? That is a question that could and should haunt our bishops and priests: if not, why not?

In our own times, missionary organizations send out compelling fundraising letters, reminding us of our obligation to provide material help to people in need. That is undeniably a part of the Christian sense of missionary work. But it is only a part. Pope Benedict XVI cautioned repeatedly that the Church is not a sort of social-welfare organization, not an NGO (non-government organization) providing humanitarian relief to the Third World. Ultimately the goal of all missionary work is to bring people closer to Christ.

Moreover, Pope Benedict XVI recognized that when Christians begin to see their missionary responsibility in purely humanitarian terms, the results are disastrous for the Faith. He said:

> It is typical that in the Church today, the more she understands herself first and foremost as an institute for social progress, the more vocations dry up—the calls to serve the old, the sick, children, and so forth; vocations that flourished so much when the Church still looked essentially to God. One could say that this is a purely empirical proof of the truth of Jesus' logion: "Seek first the Kingdom of God and his righteousness, and all the rest will be given to you" (Mt 6:33).

When Jesus sent his apostles out on their first missions,

he instructed them to care for the people they found in each town. "Heal the sick, raise the dead, cleanse lepers, drive out demons" (Mt 10:8). The best Christian missionaries have always done the same: first addressing the people's most urgent needs, then speaking to them about Christ. This is a natural progression: first to establish human contact and trust, then to reveal a great treasure. Providing food or medical attention is not a bribe or an inducement designed to provide a captive audience. It is a display of love—given freely, regardless of how the beneficiary will react. What follows is an exploration of the source of that love. We share of our substance because of our faith, and if we provide some needy people with both, the Faith is the greater gift.

Most American Catholics will never serve as missionaries in impoverished countries. But there is still poverty around us, as well as other human needs—emotional and spiritual needs—that cannot be resolved by dollar contributions. There will never be a shortage of neighbors in need. "For you always have the poor with you, and whenever you will, you can do good to them," the Lord told his disciples (Mk 14:7). Now notice how he ended that sentence: "but you will not always have me."

Unlike the seventeenth-century Jesuits, we are living in a society that has already heard the Gospel message. If we do preach the Gospel, we are usually not telling a fascinating story that our audience has never heard. Yet it should be abundantly clear to anyone who has read the day's newspaper headlines that most of our neighbors have not embraced the Faith. For that matter, a remarkable number of Americans—including educated Americans—have never actually read the Gospels and are not acquainted with the fundamentals of Christian thought. Even if a majority of Americans identify themselves as Christian, there is a great deal of evangelization still to be done. This is the purpose of the "new evangelization": to revive an active interest in the Faith in a society where interest in Christianity has waned. Evangelization is not a specialized mission to be carried out by the trained operatives, the ecclesiastical equivalent of SWAT teams. It is an everyday mission for every Christian. We may not be called to serve in the foreign missions, or even in America's inner cities. We are almost certainly not called to distribute Gospel tracts, or to proselytize door-to-door. But we are all called to do *something*. The critical question is *what* are we called to do to serve Christ and his Church in our time and place. Even if pastors and bishops are timid or vacillating in the proclamation of the Gospel, their reticence does not absolve us, as followers of Christ, from the great commission to go out and bring the good news to a world so sorely in need of it.

Evangelization can begin at home: in our families, among our neighbors and colleagues and friends. It might involve Bible studies or catechism lessons; more likely it will begin by listening, suggesting, encouraging, proposing. It may require us to overcome a certain natural reticence, to steer a friendly conversation in a direction that may prove uncomfortable. Evangelization entails taking some risks. For most of us, the risk is minor: we might be rebuffed by friends or scoffed at by skeptics. If we really do honor the martyrs—if we are not hypocrites—we surely cannot allow ourselves to be deterred by the threat of such minor injuries to our pride.

Keep in mind, too, that some risks pay off. A good sales-man learns to take rejections, confident that eventually he will make a sale. And the Christian faith does sell. Thousands of people, including many hardened cynics, are brought into the Faith every year. Father C. John McCloskey, Jr., a priest who has helped to bring many notable public figures into the Church, has revealed one secret of his success. In the course of conversation with a new acquaintance, he will find an occasion to ask, "Have you ever thought about becoming a Catholic?" The answer, he reports, is *always* yes.

Not so very long ago, thousands of young American Catholics brought converts into the Church through mar-riage. In the 1950s, 75 percent of all adult conversions in the US came about through marriages. We cannot know how many of those conversions were brought about by a genu-ine embrace of the Faith rather than a desire to smooth the approach to the wedding. And we do not know how many of those new Catholics remained active in the practice of their new faith. But we do know that the train is now running in the opposite direction. In the early years of the twenty-first century, when American Catholics marry non-Catholics, it is no longer likely that the non-Catholic will enter the Church; more often, the Catholic partner leaves.

If an American Catholic who marries a non-Catholic is likely to stop practicing the Faith—as the statistics indi-cate—that pattern forms a revealing contrast with the behavior of Catholics living under Islamic law in the Middle East. In the book *When Faith Goes Viral*, a Catholic priest who served as pastor in an Islamic country, writing under a pseudonym, described the practical problems facing his parishioners:

> *Shari'a* law forbids a Christian man from marrying a Muslim woman—in this nation, without exception—but permits a Muslim man to marry a Christian woman. Any children of their union are perforce Muslims, and must remain Muslims even after the death of their father or in the event of divorce or abandonment. The parish included a number of women married at one time to Muslims, who comprised an informal support group, seeking advice on ways to deepen their faith in the face of their husband's ridicule or the hostility of their ex-husband's in-laws. Their children sometimes accompanied them to Mass and even received Christian religious instruction, but conversion to Christianity could only take place after emigration to a non-Islamic country, and would forfeit all rights of inheritance. Few had the gumption and wherewithal to make such a radical decision. For all that, the parish contained a number of these "ghost Christians" who prayed, studied, and gave alms as Catholics—though without receiving the sacraments—yet who remained officially Muslim.

For this priest's parishioners, as for the early missionaries in North America, an open profession of the faith carried a very high cost. "Father Bashir" (as the pseudonymous author identified himself) reported that some of his most difficult hours as a pastor were spent in the confessional, helping penitents to "sort out sinful from permissible acts of evasion," as they sought to avoid calling attention to the fact that they had become Christians—an offense calling for the death penalty under Islamic law.

In February 2015, bloodthirsty militants of the Islamic State murdered a group of twenty-one Egyptians who had been living as guest workers in Libya. Twenty of the victims were Coptic Christians, who were butchered because they would not renounce their faith. The ghoulish video of the killings showed them commending their souls to the Lord before they were beheaded; they literally died with the name of Jesus on their lips. The twenty-first victim was not a Christian—until, inspired by the bravery of his comrades, he embraced the Faith and died a martyr.

Again, we Americans do not face the same sort of dire consequences for a bold proclamation of our faith. We face only various sorts of mild inconvenience when we are forthright in opposing what a majority of our countrymen have accepted. Yet how often have Catholic individuals and Catholic institutions chosen meekly to accept an evil, or tolerate a compromise, rather than risk some political or economic or social setback?

Compromise can be a good and necessary thing. Politics is, after all, the art of the possible. St. Thomas More did his best, as a prudent lawyer, to find a way to avoid overt opposition to King Henry VIII. But, finally, he determined that he could not escape the conflict without violating the principles of his faith. St. Thomas, too, became a martyr because he deemed his faith more important than his life.

St. Thomas More and St. John Fisher are justly renowned and revered, venerated to be precise, by Catholics for taking a stand, for *not* compromising their principles. They are the models for Catholic statesmen and bishops. Yet, sadly, it seems that just as the vast majority of bishops in Reformation England compromised and thus betrayed the Faith—which is to say, they betrayed Christ, for Christ can never be separated from his Church—today, too, many bishops, even otherwise good and holy men, so often and so easily compromise . . . as did a man named Cuthbert Tunstall, a man who could serve as a model for modern-day bishops.

Cuthbert Tunstall might have been a martyr too, as famous as St. Thomas More. But he made a different choice.

Like Thomas More, Cuthbert Tunstall was on intimate terms with King Henry VIII. He was not only the bishop of London but also the Lord Privy Seal. Like Thomas More, he resisted the king's divorce and paid a price for that resistance; he was exiled to the Durham diocese. But unlike Thomas More, Cuthbert Tunstall decided to cut his losses.

The moment of truth came during the controversy over the Oath of Supremacy when Cuthbert was summoned for a chat with his sovereign. King Henry's message might have gone something like this:

"Cuthbert, if you oppose me, I will have your head chopped off. I did it to Thomas More; I did it to John Fisher. Don't make me do it to you."

(It's possible, I suppose, that the king put that message in more diplomatic terms. But while Henry VIII had his faults, a tendency toward circumlocution was not one of them. He might have been even *more* direct.)

Cuthbert Tunstall found that argument compelling. He decided not to oppose the king, and he lived to a ripe old age.

As it happens, this story has a happy ending. Later in life, Bishop Tunstall regained his courage, and he *did* dare to oppose Queen Elizabeth I. He might well have become a martyr on the second go-round, but he died of natural causes before Elizabeth caught up with him.

No one has ever threatened to chop off my head. Still, I have no doubt that the threat would command my complete attention, especially if it was delivered by someone with the impeccable credibility in such matters that Henry VIII had established. So, while I do not approve of the decision Cuthbert Tunstall made after his little *tete-a-tete* with King Henry, I certainly understand it.

What I do *not* understand is the comparative ease with which American political leaders today convince Catholic leaders to mute their public criticism of immoral public policies. Many years have passed since a British prelate faced an executioner, and the American hierarchy has never had to cope with that sort of unpleasantness. Yet our Church leaders knuckle under to political pressure with an alacrity that would make the younger Cuthbert Tunstall blush.

For forty years now, prominent Catholic politicians have defied the teachings of the Church by supporting legal abortion. In the 1970s, it might have been possible for some brave bishop to discipline such a politician and thereby to persuade him to change his stance. As the years have passed, Catholic politicians have become more brazen in their defiance, and bishops even more reluctant to confront them, so that now it would take a great deal more courage for a prelate to announce that an erring public figure cannot receive the Eucharist until he repents his advocacy of the slaughter of the innocent.

Still, even today, a bishop who took that bold stand would be showing no more courage than St. Ambrose showed when he forbade Emperor Theodosius from entering a church after the slaughter of civilians at Thessalonica. The emperor held more direct power than any politician in a democratic society; he could have used that power directly against Ambrose and given the Church yet another martyr. But Theodosius did repent.

The spirit of St. Ambrose is not often visible in the Church today. Bishops are all too willing to maintain friendly ties with politicians who support the culture of death. Church-run agencies accept government contracts, becoming entangled with agencies that promote contraception and abortion abroad. Catholic charities issue grants to community organizations which, when they are not making common cause with their Catholic allies, are promoting other causes inimical to the Faith. One might argue, in any given one of such cases, that enough good is done by the charitable work to outweigh the damage caused by remote cooperation with evil. But there is a separate point to be kept in mind. If someone refuses to be involved in a questionable activity— even at cost to himself, and even when he might be able to justify his involvement—he acts as a prophetic witness.

An opportunity is lost, therefore, when a Church leader agrees to compromise even when he is not forced to do so. A pusillanimous pastor mutes the message of the martyrs, which is the message of Christ. In a dramatic address in February 1949, as the Communist regime in Hungary was subjecting the heroic Cardinal Jozef Mindszenty to a show trial, Pope Pius XII said this to an audience in St. Peter's Square:

> Do you want a Church that remains silent when she should speak; that diminishes the law of God where she is called to proclaim it loudly, wanting to accommodate it to the will of man? Do you want a Church that departs from the unshakable foundations upon which Christ founded her, taking the easy way of adapting herself to the opinion of the day; a Church that is a prey to current trends; a Church that does not condemn the suppression of conscience and does not stand up for the just liberty of the people; a Church that locks herself up within the four walls of her temple in unseemly sycophancy, forgetting the divine mission received from Christ: "Go out to the crossroads and preach to the people?" Beloved sons and daughters! Spiritual heirs of numberless confessors and martyrs! Is this the Church you venerate and love? Would you recognize in such a Church the features of your Mother? Would you be able to imagine a Successor of St. Peter submitting to such demands?[31]

Sad to say, many Catholic leaders and Catholic institutions have chosen, in our days, to accommodate themselves to the will of man. In England, for example, Bishop Kieran Conry of Arundel and Brighton announced that the adoption agency in his diocese was absolutely right to drop the word *catholic* from its name in order to survive after the government required equal treatment for same-sex couples in the adoption process. The diocesan agency could have challenged the new regulations, but Bishop Conry thought the challenge would fail. The diocese was not changing its principles, the bishop insisted, but "we're not going to have a public fight that we're possibly going to lose and come out of it with everyone suffering." He did not take into account the possibility that the diocese might actually have won a legal challenge, nor the greater likelihood that even an unsuccessful fight in court would have given the Catholic Church a chance to argue that the new policy was harmful to the interests of children.

Contrast that approach with that of the heroic Maccabees who refused to eat pork and even rejected the suggestion of sympathetic courtiers that they might escape death by *pretending* to eat pork, using some other meat. They were determined not only to preserve their ritual purity but also to send a clear message to the world about their devotion to their faith. The early Christians in Rome refused to offer sacrifices to the gods. They might have burned a bit of incense, said that it was a meaningless gesture, and spared their own lives. They did not. We—the spiritual heirs of the Maccabees, of the martyrs of Rome and of North America—should not be too quick to look for clever ways to excuse ourselves from our obligations to defend and promote the Faith.

Even less should bishops and priests do so. Even for bishops who have vacillated or compromised when they should not have in the past, it is not too late for them to become prophetic witnesses, to join the Mores and Fishers, the Maccabees and, yes, the penitent Bishop Cuthbert Tunstall.

Defending the Faith and promoting the Faith should be

recognized as two aspects of the same work. When we defend the truths of the Faith, we are giving our neighbors reasons to believe; when we promote the practice of the Faith, we are raising up new defenders. When the Faith is growing and Catholics are becoming more enthusiastic about their involvement with the Church, the civic rights of Catholics and of the Church are safer. In the matter of evangelization, the best defense is a good offense.

Defending the Faith, then, does not mean simply circling the wagons and discouraging overt attacks. In 2007, when the bishops of Latin America met at Aparecida, Brazil, to plan their "continental mission," many Catholic prelates worried aloud about the growing influence of Evangelical Protestant sects and suggested some form of government intervention to curtail the work of missionaries. The Archbishop of Buenos Aires agreed that the sects posed a worrisome challenge for the Church. But Cardinal Jorge Bergoglio, showing the enterprising, evangelical spirit that would later prompt his fellow cardinals to elect him as successor to Peter, reasoned that if the sects were making inroads among the Catholic faithful, they must be answering some need that the Catholic Church had not met. The proper response to this challenge, the future Pope Francis argued, was to redouble the evangelical efforts of the Catholic Church, to instruct the faithful more effectively, to preach the Gospel more powerfully, *not* to ask for outside help to ward off competition.

The notion that the Catholic Church requires protection so that preachers of other faiths will not steal away souls would be utterly foreign to the martyrs and the great missionaries. Think of St. Francis Xavier preaching the Gospel in India and Japan. There are dozens of good reasons why he should not have been successful, working in cultures where Christianity was unknown and other faiths were entrenched. Still, he forged ahead despite the difficulties, personally baptizing a reported three *million* people, and complaining only that he did not have enough time or enough help to reach more! If he could accomplish so much working as an alien in strange lands, surely we should be able to reach our own neighbors, who share our language and our culture and already know (even if they have not accepted) at least the rudiments of Christianity.

Maybe the story of St. Francis Xavier seems to belong in the category of "ancient history." But in more recent days, the Faith has shown the same power to transform a society, attracting new believers by the thousands. In 1900, there were only about ten million Christians in Africa, among a population of over one hundred million for the continent. Today there are over 350 million Christians, and the number is steadily growing, nearing 50 percent of the continent's total population.

When Pope Benedict XVI issued *Anglicanorum Coetibus*, establishing a framework for Anglicans who wished to enter into full communion with the Catholic Church, he was motivated by his certainty that thousands of Anglicans would be attracted to the Roman Church. (That belief was founded on strong evidence; Anglicans were banging on the doors at the Vatican, pleading for admittance.) Unfortunately, his initiative was met with resistance, especially in Great Britain. Catholic priests expressed misgivings that by encouraging Anglicans to become Catholics, the papal plan might upset the clergy of the Church of England and damage ecumenical relations. So, perversely, some Catholic priests actually discouraged a bid to bring people into the Catholic Church.

In the US, too, the Anglican ordinariates established within the Catholic Church have developed almost as a "stealth" initiative. To ensure the maximum public impact for this unprecedented gesture by Pope Benedict, the existing dioceses might have welcomed the new Anglican communities with as much publicity as possible, with brass bands and fireworks. But such celebrations could have smacked of "triumphalism;" they could have annoyed the Anglican stalwart who were accusing Catholics of "sheep-stealing." So in order to avoid offending people who are outside the Catholic family (and, by the way, often very critical of Catholic teachings), we muted our welcome for people coming *into* the fold.

The temptation to compromise when compromise is not necessary, to avoid clear statements of faith when they might cause friction, to disparage the missionary work by others, or to discourage entry into the Catholic Church is a temptation that runs directly counter to the goal of missionary work. This is anti-evangelization.

Anti-evangelization comes in a softer, more subtle form as well. While missionaries travel the world risking their lives and sometimes asking others to risk theirs as well, comfortable Catholics can settle into a routine of weekly worship, satisfying their own spiritual needs without reaching out to others. The Catholic clergyman can come see his own roles not as priest, prophet, and king but as administrator, public spokesman, fundraiser, and master-of-ceremonies at Sunday gatherings. The parish can collapse in upon itself, becoming a sort of club catering to members.

In his foreword to *The Great Commission*, by Timothy Byerley, the late Cardinal Avery Dulles pointed to evidence of that anti-evangelical strain in Catholicism: "Asked whether spreading the faith was a high priority of their parishes, 75 percent of conservative Protestant congregations and 57 percent of African American congregations responded affirmatively, whereas only 6 percent of Catholic parishes did the same. Asked whether they sponsored local evangelistic activities, 39 percent of conservative Protestant responded positively as compared with only 3 percent of Catholic parishes."

A healthy parish invites people to join the Church; a staid parish—infected by the attitudes of what Pope Francis, early in his pontificate, called the "self-referential church"—gives visitors the impression that they do not belong. An evangelical parish encourages converts; a self-referential parish might *allow* people to join the Church. If someone inquires about the Faith, he is asked to fill out forms, to join an official parish program. In the unhealthy parish, someone who takes an interest in learning more about the Faith is treated like a job applicant. ("Don't call us; we'll call you.") In a healthy parish, that same person is treated like the young woman an adult son has brought home to dinner. In the former case, the parish staff is anxious to make the newcomer conform; in the latter, the staff is anxious to meet the new arrival, learn all about her, prepare to welcome her into the family.

In a Catholic parish that has lost sight of its evangelical mission, the sacraments are still administered, the faithful are still enriched, worship is still offered, good works are still done. But something vital is missing. Parishioners may love their church and devote themselves to parish causes. But eventually, if the parish is not bringing new people into the community—including, especially, the children of the current parishioners—that love will erode into sentiment, the faith will wither, the community will shrink, the parish will close.

The decay of a healthy Catholic parish may not be evident for years, especially to the parishioners themselves. Loyal Catholics can fall into the trap of believing that because they faithfully preserve the old habits, they are fulfilling all their religious duties. Proud of their faith, they can turn away from the outside world, content with the knowledge that they have the truth and others are wrong. Conservative Catholics can be all too quick to denounce the secular world, forgetting their own obligation to change that world.

Worse still, Catholics who have lost sight of their evangelical mission can fail to convey the excitement and joy that should be characteristics of the Faith. As Pope Benedict XVI remarked, "Many people perceive Christianity as something institutional, rather than as an encounter with Christ—which explains why they don't see it as a source of joy."[32]

In a healthy Catholic community, on the other hand, parish activity is always oriented toward the goal of evangelization. When they come together for Sunday Mass, faithful Catholics are encouraged and energized to set about their business of bringing the Gospel to their neighbors. Ideally, parishioners look forward to Sunday Mass rather than thinking of their attendance as an obligation. They think of the Eucharistic liturgy as something their friends and neigh-bors would want to attend, too, if only they knew about it. That feeling, in turn, prompts them to talk to those friends and neighbors about the liturgy and thus to engage in active evangelization.

Designing an attractive liturgy can be a tricky business, however. Too often, ambitious pastors think that they can attract people to Mass by borrowing tricks from the world of entertainment: bright banners, pop music, snappy jokes in homilies. The result may be exciting to those who are directly involved in the "performance," especially at first, but eventually the shine wears off. The emphasis on "perfor-mance" is deadly to the spirit of the liturgy. The Mass should never resemble popular entertainment. The music, the ges-tures, the language, even the architecture should all serve to remind us that we are engaged in something unlike anything else we do, something "other," something holy.

In the Eucharistic liturgy, we draw inspiration not from our own actions but from the action of Jesus Christ. So it is a mistake to think that we, the faithful, are responsible for making the Mass inspirational. It is Christ's liturgy, not ours. The true spirit of the liturgy is characterized by solem-nity and reverence, by recognition that we are drawn into something utterly beyond our own powers, by a feeling of awe. That feeling of reverential awe is what draws people in to the Catholic Mass and sends them away filled with apostolic zeal.

In his perceptive book *Why Catholics Can't Sing*, Thomas Day remarked that the Catholic liturgy, especially in its pre-conciliar form, could sometimes appear as a form of withdrawal from the world. In fact, he observed, the Mass "was supposed to be liberation theology in action and slightly subversive. Far from being one form of 'opium for the people', the old High Mass was meant to be a kind of medicine that invigorated people, reminded them of their uniqueness, and sent them refreshed but determined into a hostile world."

Celebrating Mass is not just one characteristic thing that Catholics do; it is *the* thing that constitutes the Church, the source and summit of Catholic life. The way we celebrate the Eucharistic liturgy should convey—as a reminder to Catholic adults, as education to children, as a lure to visitors—that nothing else could approach the importance of this action.

The Mass is not only a community meal; it is also a sacrifice. Participating in that sacrifice, the faithful are explicitly reminded of the sacrifice of Abraham; they are reminded that they share in the faith of the prophets, the apostles, and the martyrs. (One of the most important recent changes in the life of Church has been the introduction of a new English translation of the liturgy, which revives the old language that emphasizes the continuity between Old and New Testament and underlines the sense of an eternal sacrifice.) They are reminded that they are part of a community standing outside of time. Thus, they are encouraged to recognize that they should not be ruled by the here-and-now, they should not conform themselves slavishly to the secular culture. The Mass—the worship of God, the cult—plants the seeds for a Catholic counterculture.

To sustain the faithful and to attract potential converts, the Mass should be celebrated with energy but also with great reverence. Banal liturgy, saccharine music, and distracted congregations are all deadly to the cause of evangelization. The dignity of the liturgy should convey, both to parishioners and to visitors, that something of the utmost seriousness is happening.

When the Mass is celebrated with great reverence, the beauty of the liturgy is itself a reminder that the congregation is something more than a community, the Eucharist something much more than a meal, the Catholic faith a treasure more valuable than any other. The martyrs died to bring the Eucharist, the source and summit of the Christian life, to a waiting world, fulfilling the evangelical mission that the Lord gave to his Church. If we do not do the same, we betray the martyrs.

CHAPTER 6

A Patrimony Squandered

When I first visited Rome and entered St. Peter's basilica, I was overwhelmed by two feelings, which hit me in quick succession. The first sensation was simple awe. The enormous scale of the Vatican basilica, the beauty of the architecture and the statuary, the sense of history embodied in structure, are all overwhelming, even to someone who has seen many pictures of the place. I was staggered.

As I regained my bearings, a second sensation hit me. Standing there just inside the door, at the gigantic yet graceful holy-water font, looking toward the Altar of Confession and the Bernini baldachin, I found myself thinking, with a burst of pride that caught me by surprise, "This is all mine!"

Not only mine, of course. The magnificent architecture of St. Peter's, its history and heritage, belongs to every Catholic as part of an immense patrimony bequeathed to us by our forebears in the Faith. The riches of the Faith form a priceless heritage to be shared by every Catholic. We are heirs to a great legacy, which we are obligated, as good stewards, to pass along to our children and their children. But it is also possible to squander a great legacy and so leave our children in poverty.

Christian civilization, G. K. Chesterton wrote, is a sort of "democracy of the dead." Everyone has a hand in making decisions, including the people long dead, whose actions have helped to frame the choices that we make today. One might also speak about an "economy of the dead," because what we own today, we owe in large part to the work of our ancestors. We can build on the capital they accumulated, enrich it, and hand it on to future generations with its value enhanced. Or we can fritter it away and leave our children the poorer for our sloth.

On a visit to Rome, one eventually leaves St. Peter's basilica and moves on to visit the Vatican Museums, to see some of the treasures of other civilizations. Moving through the Etruscan collection, or viewing the statues inspired by Greek mythology, one has a very different response. The artworks are beautiful, but the cultures that produced them are gone. They are memories of the past, not part of a living tradition.

Now visit the catacombs of Rome and think about the persecuted Christians who took refuge there. They are not merely historical figures for us; they are our brothers and sisters. They are the ones who have "gone before us marked with the sign of faith;" they are the martyrs we recall at every Mass, on whose prayerful help we rely to this day. They are our benefactors, whose donations—often paid in blood—support our current apostolic work.

Since we rely on the help of our fathers in faith, it is fair to say that we owe them a debt. In the Christian economy, however, we cannot satisfy the debt by repaying them. We meet our obligation by passing along the legacy of faith—enriched, ideally, but at least safely preserved—to future generations.

Even judged by purely human standards—even setting aside the immeasurable treasure that is the supernatural gift of faith—the riches of the Catholic tradition are staggering. Think about the rich literature and the oral traditions: the stories of martyrs and confessors, saints and heroes. Think of the art and architecture, the music, the poetry and drama. Take a stroll through any major public museum and notice how many of the paintings evoke themes from the Judeo-Christian tradition. Browse an anthology of poetry and see how much imagery is drawn from Christian theology—and the deeper one's knowledge of the Faith, the greater one's appreciation of the poetry.

For centuries, in Catholic schools, scholars built on the intellectual foundations that had been laid in the first universities, which were, not coincidentally, founded as centers for Christian theological inquiry. For generations, any graduate of a good Catholic liberal-arts institution would be presumed to have some knowledge of the great sweep of Western civilization and the rise of Christendom, to have read something of St. Augustine and St. Thomas Aquinas (probably in the language in which they wrote), to have an appreciation for the sacred music of Josquin and Palestrina.

Nor should our appreciation of our patrimony be limited to these highbrow heirlooms. Even poor and uneducated Catholics could draw on a rich inheritance of traditional customs, celebrations, folk tales, and popular devotions.

There was (and is, or should be) a rich texture to the life of a Christian community, with its communal feasts, its own ways of celebrating at weddings and mourning at funerals, its own favorite saints and forms of piety. Think of the two peasants bowed in prayer in Millet's painting *The Angelus* (a painting, by the way, that can only be appreciated by someone who knows the tradition of interrupting work to pray the Angelus at noon each day). They are alone, in a vast field, and their appearance suggests poverty. But, then again, they are *not* alone, because they are joined with thousands of other Catholics praying the same prayer at the same time, and they are *not* poor, because they are heirs to riches of their—our—faith.

This is the legacy that we, the living members of the Catholic faith, have inherited. We did nothing to earn it. The question is: will we protect it? Anthony Trollope devoted hundreds of pages in his Victorian novels to the plight of English noblemen worried about losing the estates that had been passed down to them; the phenomenally successful BBC series *Downton Abbey* explores the same theme. For someone who has been born into privilege, whose main task in life is to maintain the family legacy, it is a fearful disgrace to lose any part of the patrimony.

What can we say, then, about the generation of Catholics coming to age in the Western world after Vatican II? Quite suddenly, a legacy that had been built up for centuries was tossed aside. Statues and altar carvings disappeared from churches, eventually to be replaced by cheap felt banners and butcher-block tables. Popular devotions, ceremonies, and sacramentals—Benediction, forty-hours devotions, parish missions, novenas, and, yes, the Angelus—fell into disuse. The rich treasury of sacred music fell into desuetude; the old Latin of the sung liturgy seemed not to match the prosy new English translation. In Catholic schools and universities, the study of "Western Civ" yielded to contemporary social sciences. Theology students were encouraged to skip over Sts. Augustine and Aquinas, leaping directly from the Bible to the documents of Vatican II, almost as if the intervening centuries had been an intellectual embarrassment to the faithful.

The impetus for these abrupt changes did *not* come from the teachings of the council. The actual documents of Vatican II pay frequent homage to the legacy of Church teaching. The council fathers encouraged popular devotions and stressed the primacy of Gregorian chant in the Latin liturgy. The school of "new theology," which drove much of the discussion of reforms in the Catholic Church, was dedicated to *ressourcement*: a move back to the sources, back to the mainstream, of the Catholic faith. This was not an effort to reinvent Catholicism but to revitalize it, not a quest to abolish old traditions but to give them new vigor.

Unfortunately, the teachings of the council were released during a decade intoxicated by change, at a time when revolutionary movements were sweeping through the political world. Too many commentators, inside and outside the Church, happily leapt to read the council as another call for radical change. Critics of the Catholic tradition—again, both inside the Church and outside—seized the opportunity to proclaim that the world of Augustine and Aquinas, of Dante and Raphael, of incense and chant, would soon be gone forever. The treasures of the Catholic past might still be appreciated, but in museums and concert halls, by scholars and aesthetes. One thinks of the aphorism of Clarence Day:

> When eras die, their legacies
> Are left to strange police.
> Professors in New England guard
> The glory that was Greece.

The living tradition was dying out. Or so it was said. Remarkably enough, the treasures of the Catholic tradition have lived on, even if they were virtually driven underground for a while, and in the early years of the twenty-first century, they are enjoying a revival. Some parishes have learned to incorporate the musical parts of the Latin Mass into the English liturgy, and Gregorian chant has gained new popularity. Old devotions have made a comeback; in Rome, the seminarians of the North American College helped to resurrect the pious tradition of visiting the "station churches" for daily prayer during the season of Lent. In the United States, a new generation of Catholic colleges and universities, founded since the council, has produced graduates who are conversant with the great sweep of the Catholic intellectual tradition. Pope Benedict XVI did an immeasurable service to the recovery, first by allowing broader access to the traditional Latin liturgy, and then by welcoming former Anglicans into the Catholic Church and encouraging their use of a liturgy drawn from the Book of Common Prayer. In the summer and fall of 2018, the traditional "ember days" of fasting made a comeback, with hundreds of American

Catholics observing them for the first time, as a way of doing special penance for the welfare of their beleaguered Church.

Still, it would be foolishly optimistic to exaggerate the breadth of this revival; it has not yet reached the typical American parish. Here and there, good Catholic individuals and families and institutions are dusting off the heirloom china and shining the silverware of our religious legacy. We can, with a little effort, ensure that we ourselves, and our children, enjoy the rich benefits of our patrimony. But we definitely cannot take it for granted that our neighbors, or our children's friends, or their future spouses, will have the same benefits. For a nobleman, to be a good steward involves not only preserving the family's estate but also providing some benefits for the ordinary people of the surrounding town. For us as Catholics, there is a great deal of work to be done before we can say that we have been good stewards.

Incidentally, the general appreciation of our Catholic heritage began to lag at roughly the same time that the American birth rate went into a steep decline, eventually dipping below the "replacement rate" at which population would hold steady without immigration. Is it surprising that we, as a people, stopped thinking so much about what we would pass along to our children, during the same years that we stopped having so many children—that we turned our attention away from our heritage, as we chose not to have so many heirs?

In a brilliant essay[33] published in the October 2013 issue of *First Things*, the French scholar Remi Brague argues that the rise of secularism is incompatible with a vigorous and lasting culture. (The very term *secular*, he observes, has very distinctively Christian roots. Ironically, the word originally referred to the "secular" clergy: ordinary diocesan priests, as opposed to members of religious orders.) The word itself is derived from the Latin *saeculum*, which gives us the word *century*. And that is appropriate, Brague argues, because a century—roughly the maximum span of a human life—is the attention span of a secular "culture." The secular society, in other words, does not look to the future, does not build an endowment for future generations, indeed does not produce offspring to keep the enterprise going.

Contrast that truncated vision of our role in history with that of an ancient culture. For the Spartans who fought at Thermopylae, the greatest possible good was to be remembered by future generations for military prowess and bravery. Say what you will about the perverse brutality of Spartan culture, but the warriors at Thermopylae achieved their goal. They not only stalled the Persian conquest of Greece but also wrote their names indelibly on the pages of history so that twenty-five hundred years later, we say the name "Leonidas" with respect—exactly as he wished!

We can respect the Spartan warriors, even as we shudder at their obsession with warfare, because we recognize that they were true to their beliefs. By the same token, many non-Catholics have come to admire the Church and her traditions without necessarily accepting the Catholic faith. For example, the novelist Willa Cather wrote to a sociologist explaining that although she regularly treated Catholic themes, she was not a Catholic. She continued, "On the other hand, I do not regard the Roman Church as merely 'artistic material.' If the external form and ceremonial of that Church happens to be more beautiful than that of other churches, it certainly corresponds to some beautiful vision within. It is sacred, if for no other reason than that it is the faith that has been most loved by human creatures, and loved over the greatest stretch of centuries."

Many years earlier, in 1774, John Adams wrote to his wife, Abigail, to describe the beauty of the ceremony he had observed when he visited a parish church in Philadelphia:

> This afternoon, led by curiosity and good company, I strolled away to mother church, or rather grandmother church. I mean the Romish chapel. I heard a good, short moral essay upon the duty of parents to their children, founded in justice and charity, to take care of their interests, temporal and spiritual. This afternoon's entertainment was to me most awful and affecting; the poor wretches fingering their beads, chanting Latin, not a word of which they understood; their pater nosters and ave Marias; their holy water; their crossing themselves perpetually; their bowing to the name of Jesus, whenever they hear it; their bowings, kneelings and genuflections before the altar. The dress of the priest was rich white lace. His pulpit was velvet and gold. The altar-piece was very rich, little images and crucifixes about; wax candles lighted up. But how shall I describe the picture of our Savior in a frame of marble over the altar, at full length, upon the cross in the agonies, and the blood dropping and streaming from his wounds! The music, consisting of an organ and a choir of singers, went all the afternoon except

sermon time, and the assembly chanted most sweetly and exquisitely. Here is everything which can lay hold of the eye, ear, and imagination–everything which can charm and bewitch the simple and ignorant. I wonder how Luther ever broke the spell.

Adams—a believing Christian, but a product of his New England Puritan background, and surely no friend of the Catholic Church—describes the scene with some disdain, yet cannot conceal his admiration for a rite that employs "everything which can lay hold of the eye, ear, and imagination." (He would later help organize a drive to raise funds for Boston's first Catholic cathedral.) Is it likely that a Protestant guest happening upon a Mass at an ordinary Catholic parish today would have the same sense that the liturgy was captivating? If a Catholic from the parish that Adams visited could travel in time from 1774 to the present, would he think that the Catholic liturgy had been enriched?

Understand, now, that the beauty of the liturgical rubrics, the music, and the architecture are not the greatest treasures of the Church. Active Catholics should shy away from the attitudes of aesthetes who want old churches preserved only for their historic and cultural value, or so that they can be used for organ concerts. Nor should we even encourage people to focus on those aspects of Catholic life if they distract attention from the focus on Christ. The feminist social critic Camille Paglia, now a professed atheist, notes that in her youth she was entranced by nearly everything about Catholicism except the faith itself: "I loved the cult of saints, the bejeweled ceremonialism, the eerie litanies of Mary—all the things, in other words, that Martin Luther and the other Protestant reformers rightly condemned as medieval Romanist intrusions into primitive Christianity."[34]

Still, while the sacrifice of the Mass should always be the central focus of attention in a Catholic church, the beauty of the setting can help the faithful to pray, inspiring devotion and bringing distracted minds back to the business at hand. The music and the architecture were developed to provide the most appropriate, reverent setting for the liturgy. When the music and architecture are slapdash and formulaic, it is a sign that the approach to the liturgy is equally banal.

In his important book *The Stripping of the Altars,* Eamon Duffy shows that during the English Reformation, Henry VIII and his successors suppressed a previously healthy Church by abolishing Catholic traditions. The altars were stripped again in the latter part of the twentieth century, not by any hostile force outside the Church, but by subversion from within. The material damage done to churches by heedless, self-important advocates of "reform"—who removed and discarded statues and altar rails and stained-glass windows and confessional booths and votive candles and tabernacles and vestments and monstrances—could be measured in many millions of dollars. The spiritual and culture costs of that religious vandalism were incalculable.

This "stripping of the altars," too, occurred in the years following Vatican II, not because it was mandated by the council, but because devotion to the riches of the Catholic tradition had already begun to fade. In most American parishes, in the years before the council, there was little Gregorian chant, still less polyphonic sacred music, and a great number of saccharine hymns sung by the warbling voices of untrained choirs. As for the architecture of the parishes built just before Vatican II, Thomas Day wrote in *Why Catholics Can't Sing*, "By the 1950s the religion which had defied the laws of gravity with Chartres cathedral and had lovingly adorned parish churches with great artworks was now constructing grim warehouses for worship. . . . Nobody wanted to be accused of wasting the church's resources and taking funds away from parochial schools."

In the 1950s, the great Catholic building spree was designed to produce a "parish plant," with each church flanked by a rectory and a parochial school, and a convent full of teaching sisters to staff that school located around the corner. That model, promising a Catholic bastion in every town, proved unreachable in the years after the council. But the building campaign may have been the last stage of a larger historical trend that had already run its course within the Church.

In *Evangelical Catholicism*, George Weigel argues persuasively that during the long pontificate of Leo XIII (from 1878 to 1903), the Catholic Church gradually began a shift away from the pastoral practices that had prevailed since the Council of Trent in the mid-1500s. At Trent, Weigel explains, the Protestant Reformation was the greatest challenge to the Faith, and the council fathers prescribed a response that emphasized theological orthodoxy, personal piety, and the establishment of distinctively Catholic institutions. That formula worked wonderfully for generations, unleashing the power of the Counter-Reformation and bringing new vigor to the life of the Church. But over the centuries, the movement lost its initial energy and purpose. The reforms begun by the leaders of the Counter-Reformation became settled patterns, a familiar way of life, which could easily become a routine.

Thus, the vigorous defense of the Faith eventually deteriorated into what might simply be characterized as a defensive attitude. In his book *The Decline and Fall of the Catholic Church in America*, David Carlin makes a point that resonates with Weigel's historical analysis:

> One of the great hymns of the Reformation was Martin Luther's "A Mighty Fortress Is Our God." In its reaction to the Reformation, Catholicism might well have taken the title of this hymn for its own slogan— for that is what the Church became: it turned itself, metaphorically speaking, into a mighty ecclesiastical fortress. Eventually it recognized that the chances of regaining most of the lost provinces were slim, but it was absolutely determined to hold on to what remained: France, Spain, Portugal, Italy, southern Germany, Poland, Ireland, and (an area of great new gains) Latin America. This siege mentality prevailed in the Counter-Reformation Church—a mentality that placed primary importance on survival.

The fortress mentality exercised enormous influence on the Church in the United States, where Catholics were always a minority, anxious to gain acceptance in a predominantly Protestant society. Ambitious Church leaders sought to build up their parishes, parochial schools, Catholic universities, and lay associations, for whose use the "parish plants" were built. With each succeeding generation, the Catholic Church became a more entrenched institution, with all the benefits—but also the dangers—of acceptance as part of the established American way of life.

In *The Cost of Discipleship*, Dietrich Bonhoeffer lamented that the Christian community in Germany, by pursuing the comfort of the establishment and failing to make stronger demands on the faithful, helped to ease the resistance to the Nazi regime. Bonhoeffer's criticism was aimed at the Lutheran Church in Germany, but his critique might be applied to American Catholicism as well: "We gave away the word and sacraments wholesale, we baptized, confirmed, and absolved a whole nation unasked and without condition. . . . But the call to follow Jesus in the narrow way was hardly ever heard."

The desire to fit comfortably into the routines of American life was sometimes reflected in a casual or routinized approach to the liturgy. Today's proponents of the traditional Latin liturgy extol the beauty of the Tridentine ritual, and rightly so. But in the years before the council, in a typical American parish, that ancient liturgy was too often approached haphazardly, celebrated carelessly, treated as an obligation to be rushed through as quickly as possible. After the council, of course, the introduction of a new streamlined liturgy gave immeasurably more scope to the casual approach. In *Why Catholics Can't Sing*, Thomas Day comments:

> We can be reasonably sure that the Last Supper did not begin with the words, "Good evening, apostles."

Intuition tells us that John the Baptist did not cry out in the wilderness, "Repent, sin no more, and havernice day." Common sense tells us that there is something immensely wrong and contradictory about starting off a ritual with "Good Morning." We might even say that the laity in the pews "short circuits" when greeted this way at Mass. The church building, the music, and the celebrant in flowing robes all seem to say, "This is a ritual," an event out of the ordinary. Then, the "Good Morning" intrudes itself and indicates that this is really a business meeting and not a liturgy, after all.

Today, after more than a full generation of liturgical experimentation, the integrity of the liturgy can be compromised by two opposite dangers: caring too little about the established rubrics or caring too much. Some priests are too relaxed, even sloppy, in their approach to the liturgy (and this is by far the more common problem), while others are too eager to try out their own "creative" new ideas, or too punctilious about the niceties of the ritual. Either error reflects the mistaken assumption that the Eucharistic liturgy is about "us," the priest-celebrant and the congregation, rather than about Christ's Sacrifice on Calvary. The focus on the here-and-now—whether it is motivated by a desire to move things along quickly and satisfy the customers or by an urge to stir up new emotional enthusiasm—diverts attention from the precious *gift* of the liturgy.

Since Vatican II, proponents of liturgical reform have argued that the old approach to the liturgy, with its subtle gestures and quiet chants, was not accessible to the majority of Catholics. To encourage more active participation, they said, the liturgy should be made more relevant, more attractive. In practice, however, there is precious little evidence that the new approach has produced any greater degree of participation; in most parishes, the ordinary people in the pews remain as silent as ever. Moreover, the historical record suggests that more people are attracted to the Church when the demands placed on the faithful are greatest. It is worth keeping in mind that the early centuries of Christianity, when discipline was strictest and non-believers were kept out of churches, were also the years of the fastest growth in the numbers of the faithful.

Ideally the liturgy should be a natural, organic expression of faith, reflecting the desire of the Catholic community to worship God, and reflecting, too, the desire to conform that act of worship to the ancient patterns of the Faith. The ritual, like the words of the Eucharistic Prayers, should remind the faithful that they stand in the tradition of Abraham and Isaac, of the apostles and martyrs. In a sense, the liturgy, like every other aspect of Christian life, should tap into the same aquifers of faith that have nourished the life of the Church throughout the ages. The Church is run by sinners like you and me: error-prone human beings who never get anything quite right. Still, for all our faults, we Catholics have amassed a prodigious store of treasures: spiritual, physical, artistic, and educational. Now that precious heritage is in jeopardy.

Consider, for a moment, just the physical resources built up by faithful Catholics in America over the years. Scrimping and saving so that they could contribute their hard-earned nickels and dimes, working-class Catholics bequeathed us beautiful churches, parish schools, hospitals, and universities. Now many of those churches and schools are closed, while the hospitals are being sold off to secular corporations. We cannot ignore the spending of over $3 billion to pay the costs incurred by an inexcusable failure to curb sexual abuse among the clergy—a squandering of resources that has now driven ten dioceses into bankruptcy.

Parish closings are commonplace in America today, and prelates are praised for their smooth handling of what is seen as an "inevitable" contraction of the Church. A question for the bishops who subscribe to such a defeatist view. *Why is it inevitable?*

The closing of a parish is an admission of defeat. If the faithful could support a parish on this site at one time, why can they not support a parish today? American cities are dotted with magnificent church structures, built with the nickels and dimes that hard-pressed immigrant families could barely afford to donate. Today the affluent grandchildren of those immigrants are unwilling to keep current with the parish fuel bills and, more to the point, to encourage their sons to consider a life of priestly ministry.

There are times, admittedly, when parishes are doomed by demographic shifts. There are city neighborhoods in which two Catholic churches were built, literally across the street from one another: one for the benefit of French-speaking families, the other for their German-speaking neighbors. Such cases, however, account for only a small proportion of the parish closings that we see in the US today. More typically, the parish slated for closing is located in a comfortable, populous neighborhood, with no other Catholic church particularly close at hand and no special reason why the community that supported a thriving parish in 1960 cannot maintain the same parish now, fifty years later. No reason, that is, except the decline of the Catholic faith. Parishes close because Catholic families don't care enough about the Faith to keep them open.

Why *don't* families care enough? Why is there such a widespread indifference to the treasures of the Catholic faith? At least one powerful factor is surely the attitude that lay Catholics have observed in their priests and their bishops. If the clergy, the stewards of the patrimony, are content to act as bystanders as the Catholic patrimony is degraded, their indifference becomes infectious.

In other instances, the parishes close because although the neighborhood is still populous, the Catholic families have moved out and the new residents come from different religious backgrounds or come without religious beliefs. In such cases, we are told, the Church must accept the new reality and realize that the neighborhood cannot support a parish. But why make such a concession? Why should we admit that it is impossible to convert the new residents to our faith? A Catholic fired with apostolic zeal, discovering a neighborhood in which the population is mostly non-Catholic, should set out to convert the people, not to close the church. In at least a few cases with which I am personally familiar, parishioners have asked their bishop to leave the parish open for a few years to give them an opportunity to build up a new model of evangelical outreach, to bring new converts into the parish and make it financially viable once again. When those appeals have been rejected, the parishioners have concluded, not illogically, that their bishop does not share their trust in the winning power of the Gospel.

When St. Patrick, having escaped slavery in Ireland, arrived again as a missionary, the country was pagan. By the time he died, the country was Catholic. He came into a "neighborhood"—an entire nation—that could not support a parish. But he did not accept what lesser souls might have considered inevitable. Instead, he changed the conditions of the neighborhood, and soon a parish was created. And another and another and another. During his years of ministry in the once-pagan country, he is said to have consecrated over three hundred bishops. In Ireland today there are seven dioceses—not parishes, dioceses—that trace their foundation to St. Patrick's missionary work.

If as a bishop and missionary St. Patrick could convert an entire nation, why can't his successors at least strive to match his success? We have material advantages that would have left St. Patrick gasping: the ability to travel hundreds of miles in a day, the capacity for instant communication across the globe. Is the content of the Catholic faith less viable today than it was in the fifth century? Is the guidance of the Holy Spirit less valuable? I know how St. Patrick would answer those questions.

CHAPTER 7

The Worst of Both Worlds

If you are going to be hanged as a horse thief anyway, the old adage tells us, you might as well steal a horse.

Over the course of the past generation, the Church has been vilified for attempting to impose sectarian norms on secular society. Yet the historical record shows no successful campaigns to enact Catholic morality into law in the United States: none. We have been blamed for doing something that we did not do—indeed, rarely attempted to do.

Catholic activists have always insisted that the laws they seek to enact or preserve—such as laws protecting innocent human life, or those defining marriage as a lifetime union between a man and a woman—reflect moral norms that can be explained without reference to any specific religious beliefs, norms that are inscribed on the human heart. So Catholics engaged in public debate, acting from the best of motives, have sought to couch their arguments in purely secular terms.

Ironically, Catholics might have had more success in the

world of politics if, instead of trying to make moral norms more palatable to a secular audience, we had devoted our attention to turning secularists into Catholics—putting our primary emphasis on religious conversions and letting political matters take care of themselves. We thought we were following a subtle strategy, hoping to change minds without first changing hearts. But that approach has failed. Pure evangelization would have been more effective, even from a purely political perspective.

In September 2013, Pope Francis caused an international sensation when, in an interview that appeared simultaneously in several Jesuit publications, he said that the Catholic Church "cannot insist only on issues related to abortion, gay marriage, and the use of contraceptive methods." Instead, he proposed, the Church should emphasize "what fascinates and attracts more, what makes the heart burn."

"We have to find a new balance," the pontiff said. He did *not* say that the Church should cease to defend the right to life and the integrity of marriage. But he argued that in order to draw people toward Christ—in order to persuade people that they should listen to the voice of the Church—Catholics must first capture the public's attention. In a society full of people with urgent material and emotional needs, Pope Francis said, the first priority for the Church is to provide help and hope. Likening the Church to a "field hospital" treating gravely wounded patients, he said, "You have to heal his wounds. Then we can talk about everything else."

To the ears of the secular world, the pope's remarks sounded very much like a call for truce in the "culture wars." Hundreds of op-ed columns were produced congratulating the pontiff on his call for an end to the Catholic "obsession" with issues of sexuality. The National Abortion and Reproductive Rights Action League (NARRAL) actually produced an advertisement thanking the pope for his words—surely the first time the group had welcomed any statement by a Roman pontiff. Pro-life activists, on the other hand, were deflated by the pope's words, feeling that he had undercut their efforts and belittled their sacrifices.

But amid the furor created over the pope's words, one crucial question was ignored: when and where (if ever) had the Church tried to "insist only on issues related to abortion, gay marriage, and the use of contraceptive methods"? Certainly that has not been the case in the United States.

Yes, it is true that when leaders of the Catholic Church have appeared in the secular news headlines recently, they have frequently been speaking on these topics (or on that other favorite topic of the secular media, the sexual abuse of children by Catholic priests). But have those headlines reflected an obsession on the part of Catholic bishops, or the selective interests of the secular media?

At the grassroots level—that is, in the lives of typical Catholic parishes—the culture wars rarely play an important role. Catholics who attend Mass every Sunday can testify that it is rare to hear a homily that mentions abortion, contraception, or homosexuality. Catholic bishops might draw headlines when they issue a strong condemnation of abortion in an address to an audience of pro-life activists, but they are not likely to deliver the same strong message to a neutral audience: a parish confirmation class, perhaps, or at a fundraising luncheon for Catholic Charities.

If there is one issue on which the teachings of the Catholic Church are most dramatically at odds with the common morality of Americans today, it is the issue of contraception. The Church is widely recognized as the single major institution that continues to oppose the use of artificial birth control. Everyone knows that the Catholic Church regards contraception as a grave evil. Everyone also knows that despite the Church teaching, at least 90 percent of Catholic couples use contraception. Yet in my entire adult life—which roughly coincides with the years since Pope Paul VI reaffirmed the traditional Catholic teaching in 1968 with his encyclical *Humanae Vitae*—I have never once heard contraception condemned in a homily at an ordinary Sunday Mass in an ordinary parish church.

Now consider what it means that most members of an institution would continue in a practice that the institution denounces. Of course the Church denounces sin, and all Catholics remain sinners. But contraception is a different matter because conscientious Catholics recognize their sins as wrong, the consequences of their own weaknesses, whereas most married Catholics, when polled, assert that they see no moral problem with the use of contraceptives. Clearly the Church has failed to communicate a convincing case against contraception to the vast majority of her own faithful.

If "everyone knows" that the Church sees contraception as gravely wrong and yet "everyone knows" that most Catholics persist in using birth control, the Catholic community is exposed to charges of hypocrisy. Observers might easily conclude—in fact do regularly conclude—that the Church is an institution that does not mean what she says.

Moreover, critics of Catholicism are encouraged to believe that Church leaders have not made a convincing case because there is no convincing case to be made. The silence of the Church—at the practical level, the parish level—suggests to the world that the Church cannot persuade and must therefore rely only on the enforcement of arbitrary rules. If the only clear expressions of opposition to contraception come from Rome, it may seem that the Vatican is imposing a rule by the sheer force of authority, without a reasoned explanation.

From outside, the Catholic Church is perceived as obsessed with issues of sexual morality and intent on imposing sectarian rules on society at large. From inside, active Catholics only infrequently hear these issues mentioned. They may read about formal statements issued by bishops, usually to friendly audiences. But the condemnations of abortion and same-sex marriage—to say nothing of contraception—are not translated into action at the grassroots level.

In a candid conversation with the *Wall Street Journal's* James Taranto in 2012, Cardinal Timothy Dolan of New York admitted that the publication of *Humanae Vitae* "brought such a tsunami of dissent, departure, disapproval of the Church, that I think most of us—and I'm using the first-person plural intentionally, including myself—kind of subconsciously said: 'Whoa. We'd better never talk about that, because it's just too hot to handle.'" The cardinal acknowledged the result: "We forfeited the chance to be a coherent moral voice when it comes to one of the more burning issues of the day."[35]

The notion that the contraception issue is "too hot to

handle" is a self-reinforcing argument. If one generation of pastors ducks the issue, the next generation will find it all the more difficult to open the discussion. If bishops had threatened disciplinary sanctions on Catholic politicians who promoted abortion in the early 1980s, they might have been able to change the course of American history. After decades of silence, they cannot expect obedience now; the acceptance of legal abortion is too thoroughly entrenched.

Several American bishops have won reputations as ardent pro-life advocates—to be embraced by those on one side of the political debate, and vilified by those on the other— solely on the basis of their strongly worded speeches to sympathetic audiences at the local right-to-life assemblies. For pro-lifers, the tough-talking bishop is a source of inspiration and leadership. For abortion advocates, he is an equally welcome villain, who can be portrayed in fundraising letters as a dire threat to a woman's free access to abortion. Neither side has any great interest in noticing whether the bishop or his diocese actually *do* anything, on the practical level, to oppose the abortion industry or even to encourage other Catholics to join in the political struggle to protect innocent human life.

So the Church today suffers the worst of both worlds: condemned for using strong-arm political tactics while in fact being politically ineffectual and criticized for obsession with the culture wars while actually abstaining from the crucial battles.

How did this happen? How did such a wide discrepancy arise between the public perception of the Catholic Church and actual pastoral practices? There are at least three reasons.

First, since the time of the Enlightenment, secular liberals have rightly seen Catholicism as their most powerful enemy. Voltaire's famous rallying cry, "*Ecrasez l'infame!*" was directed against the Catholic Church. The goal of secularists is not merely to reduce the influence of religious faith but to crush it utterly. Whether the political battle of the day involves the power of the monarchy or control of the schools or sexual behavior, the Catholic Church is always the enemy. The American secular media, with a long history of genteel anti-Catholic bias, happily cooperate with campaigns to portray the Church as socially backward.

Second, many Catholics have distanced themselves from the Church because of their involvement, or the involvement of someone close to them, in abortion or contraception or an illicit marriage or a homosexual affair. They are now stung by the knowledge that they failed to meet the standards of the Church that nurtured them. From their perspective, the single dominant issue in their fractured relationship with the Church is a question of sexual morality. So—even if they never heard the issue discussed in their parish church, even if no one connected with the Church ever rebuked them—they know, as "everyone knows," that they are at odds with the teachings of the Church that nourished them. They are quite ready to support the notion that the Church is "obsessed" with these issues because, in a sense, *they* are.

Third, and most important, lay Catholics have been very prominent in the public opposition to legal abortion and to same-sex marriage, and even if they have not received strong support from their own pastors, they have drawn heavily on official statements from the Vatican and from the US bishops' conference to support their arguments. In the context of the American political scene, the defenders of human life and of marriage have allied themselves with the Republican Party. Consequently, liberal critics of the Church, seeing quotations from the US bishops' statement in the pro-life literature, charge that the Catholic hierarchy has aligned itself with the Republicans. Meanwhile, ardent pro-lifers, frustrated that they have not received *more* practical support from the hierarchy, and noticing the many statements from the US bishops' conference supporting Democratic stands on issues such as immigration and health-care policy and welfare spending, firmly believe that the bishops are allied with the Democrats. Once again the bishops find themselves in the worst of all possible situations: both liberal Democrats and conservative Republicans think of the Catholic hierarchy as allied with their opponents!

The charge that Catholic bishops are meddling in partisan political affairs is not a new development arising in the twenty-first century. Writing in the *New York Times* in February 1990, Arthur Schlesinger, Jr., complained that leading prelates like New York's Cardinal John O'Connor seemed to be "doing their best to verify the fears long cherished by the No-Nothings [*sic*] in the 1850s, the Ku Klux Klan in the 1920s, and a succession of anti-Catholic demagogues that the Roman Catholic Church would try to overrule the American democratic process." Schlesinger himself had once written that anti-Catholicism was the "last acceptable prejudice" among American intellectuals. Yet here he was invoking that prejudice himself. Virulent anti-Catholics of earlier generations had encouraged the belief that American Catholics would seize their first opportunity to install "the Pope of Rome" as ruler over the United States. Opposition to the campaign of the first Catholic candidate for the White House, Al Smith, crystallized around that fear in 1928. In 1950, Paul Blanshard revived the same sort of fear with his book *American Freedom and Catholic Power*. Now Schlesinger was making the same complaint that Catholic prelates were trying to write Roman dogma into American law.

An important distinction should be made here. Cardinal O'Connor and his auxiliary, Bishop Austin Vaughan, had invoked Schlesinger's wrath by warning certain Catholic politicians living in the New York archdiocese (Geraldine Ferraro and Mario Cuomo) that they were distancing themselves from the Catholic Church by their support for legal abortion. In doing so, these prelates were speaking as pastors to members of their flock. They were not demanding that secular legislatures adopt Catholic moral laws; they were admonishing individual Catholics to adhere to the teachings of the Faith they professed. But that distinction was lost on liberal American commentators.

To be fair, American Catholic bishops had not always maintained that distinction carefully during the decade leading up to Schlesinger's lament. During the 1980s, as the pro-life movement took root, the US bishops' conference became heavily involved in a debate over whether the effects of the *Roe v. Wade* decision should be reversed by a legislative act or a constitutional amendment. The bishops' direct involvement in that debate was imprudent; bishops have no special expertise on questions of practical politics, and the net result of their intervention was to exacerbate divisions within the pro-life movement, harming the chances for passage of *either* the constitutional amendment or the legislative act.

When they voiced their opinions on the appropriate political strategy for the pro-life movement, the leaders of the US bishops' conference took it for granted that lay Catholics—who dominated the leadership of the movement—would accept their authority. That was a serious miscalculation. In an era marked by dissent, bishops cannot assume that their voices will carry the debate even on matters of doctrine when they really do speak as authoritative teachers of the Catholic faith. Still less can they assume that their voices will prevail in public arguments when non-Catholics must be convinced and the bishops cannot claim any special grace of state. The bishops could cite Church teachings against abortion, but they could not thereby sway the debate in the political world. As George Weigel observes in *Evangelical Catholicism*, "The phrase 'The Church teaches . . .' means nothing outside the Church. It also means much less than it should inside the Church."

As long as the Catholic hierarchy commanded the assent of the faithful, the bishops carried a great deal of political clout. Even if they found the Catholic arguments unconvincing, politicians realized that the bishops could sway an enormous bloc of voters. But when theological dissent became commonplace in the wake of the Second Vatican Council—with *Humanae Vitae* becoming the focal point for the most heated intramural disputes—politicians realized that the bishops were no longer the undisputed leaders of the Catholic voting bloc.

The American bishops clung to their authority, issuing statements to reaffirm the Church's teachings on abortion. But as the years passed, the bishops' failure to mobilize the faithful—or even to mobilize pastors in their own dioceses—became increasingly evident. Prominent Catholic politicians who flouted the Church's teachings and voted to support legal abortion faced no disciplinary consequences. Although tens of thousands of earnest Catholics became active in the pro-life movement, most parish communities remained on the sidelines. Politicians, who are adept at counting votes, came to realize that the Catholic bishops controlled few votes aside from their own.

In the absence of a concerted effort to encourage pro-life activism at the parish level and to rebuke Catholics who support the "culture of death," the steady stream of statements from the hierarchy began to ring hollow. Taken by themselves, the formal pronouncements from the bishops' conference were strong and clear, repeating and explaining the Church's unswerving condemnation of unrestricted abortion. But those statements could *not* be taken by themselves; they formed only a part of a broader picture in which Americans generally saw a divergence of opinion among people who identified themselves as faithful Catholics.

When they issued statements that reaffirmed what "the Church teaches" about abortion (and later, about other neuralgic or hot-button issues), the American bishops inadvertently contributed to the perception of "the Church" as some distant body—at the Vatican, perhaps—that sets arbitrary policies. Public statements from the episcopal conference often failed to convey any idea that the bishops *themselves* were teaching or that they were outraged, and lay Catholics should be outraged, by the betrayal of prominent Catholics who failed to uphold the dignity of human life.

In making this argument, I do not mean to imply that Church leaders used only arguments from authority in making the case against abortion. On the contrary, the best statements from the bishops' conference deliberately crafted the pro-life message in terms that anyone, Catholic or not, could accept. From Rome, Pope John Paul II made a powerful case—most notably in his encyclical *Evangelium Vitae*—that the arguments set forth by the Church were based on natural law, engraved on the human soul, accessible to anyone willing to reason through the issues. But the urgency of the statements from the Catholic hierarchy was not matched by similarly urgent activity at the diocesan or parish level. The arguments issued by "the Church" seemed to be at odds with the actual experiences of ordinary Catholics. In other words, the bishops seemed to "talk a good game."

During the last few presidential election campaigns, American bishops have been caught up in debates over whether Catholic politicians who support the "culture of death" should be barred from receiving Communion. Those debates have generated a great deal of coverage in the secular media, creating the widespread impression that the hierarchy is cracking down on pro-abortion Catholics. Yet only once or twice has a prominent politician been told that he or she should not approach for Communion, and never, to my knowledge, has a leading Catholic political figure been actually denied the Eucharist. Yet again the Church has the worst of two worlds: an unpopular perception and an unpleasant reality. The public believes that the bishops have moved forcefully to quash dissent, yet in practice the dissenters grow ever bolder in their defiance of the bishops' authority.

For thirty years, pro-life advocates have been pleading for greater clarity from the American hierarchy. "You can't be Catholic and pro-choice," the popular bumper sticker proclaims. Yet some of the nation's most prominent Catholic politicians—the late Senator Ted Kennedy, former vice president Joe Biden, former speaker of the house Nancy Pelosi—have been outspoken proponents of unrestricted legal abortion. Pro-lifers have begged bishops to enforce canon 915 of the Code of Canon Law, a canon that obliges priests to protect the Church from scandal by withholding the Eucharist from unrepentant public sinners. Most bishops have demurred. As noted earlier, the disgraced former cardinal McCarrick, famously remarked that he would not be "comfortable" invoking the Church's law in such cases.

For the Catholic Church and for the cause of life, however, the frustration of the pro-life movement is only one sign of a deeper problem. It is true that the American bishops have failed to exercise appropriate ecclesiastical discipline, and it is true that this failure has aggravated the difficulty. But ultimately, the problem is not a failure to enforce rules. The problem is the yawning gap between the formal statements of the hierarchy and the actual behavior of most Catholics. The problem is that after issuing admirable statements about the dignity of human life, our Church leaders, as a group, have not worked assiduously to build up support for the Gospel of Life among the Catholic faithful, let alone in society at large. Regrettably, most Church leaders have treated the "culture wars" debates—abortion and homosexuality and contraception and euthanasia and embryo research—as political issues to be managed, or debating issues to be mastered, rather than as challenges for evangelization.

In the context of a public controversy, what does it mean to say that the Church holds a certain position if the Catholic people do not confirm that belief by their own actions? The American bishops have issued statements chastising Catholic politicians who support the culture of death and warned that these Catholics have separated themselves from the community of the faithful. But where is the outward evidence of that separation? How often have bishops *named* the politicians who have transgressed, or met with them privately to warn them about the eternal consequences of their actions? Or, to look at the question from the opposite perspective, how often have bishops appeared at public functions, smiling and shaking hands with the politicians whose public stands they have denounced as repugnant? How many parishes, Catholic schools, and diocesan charities have welcomed pro-abortion speakers to their fundraising events, and even conferred accolades upon them?

To keep things in perspective, we should realize that the Church has confronted these problems in the past. Our problems are not new; our Church has survived similar difficulties. Sixteen centuries ago, St. Augustine lamented, "And so in our own times: many forms of sin, though not just the same as those of Sodom and Gomorrah, are now so openly and habitually practiced, that not only dare we not excommunicate a layman, we dare not even degrade a clergyman, for the commission of them."

At a minimum, Catholics who flout the Church's teachings on key moral issues should feel uncomfortable attending Mass. In a sense, all Catholics should have a keen sense of their own unworthiness; thus in the Byzantine liturgy the faithful repeatedly chant, "Lord have mercy," as they approach the Eucharist. But in particular, Catholics who are in open defiance of Church teaching should feel the prick of conscience. And clergymen who are not willing to uphold Catholic teachings should feel the even more acute discomfort of someone who is known to be a hypocrite. Catholic politicians who support the "culture of death" should find their vote totals plummeting in Catholic neighborhoods. They should find that their fellow parishioners shun them, or better, remonstrate with them at every opportunity, seeking to show them the error of their ways. If a politician who supports abortion persists in receiving Communion, perhaps some other members of his parish should abstain, demonstrating that they are not "in communion" with him. None of these things has happened.

If politicians who support the culture of death truly have separated themselves from the Catholic community—and they have—then why is the separation not evident to the public? Because there has not been a concerted effort to teach the Catholic faithful and, more important, to motivate them for action in defense of life. There have been many formal reminders of what the Church teaches, but few efforts to show, by precept and by example, that individual Catholics can be held accountable for not honoring the Church's teachings. One noteworthy exception would be the column written by Archbishop Joseph Naumann for the *Kansas City Star* in March 2009 explaining that he had instructed Governor Kathleen Sebelius (who at the time was President Obama's nominee to become Secretary of Health and Human Services) not to receive Communion because of her public support for legal abortion. The archbishop explained:

> Catholics have a personal responsibility not to receive Holy Communion if they have with knowledge and intention committed a grave evil. . . . For more than 25 years, Gov. Sebelius has advocated and supported legalized abortion. She has opposed such modest protections as parental notification for minors, waiting periods, informed consent and improved regulation of abortion clinics. In the hope to awaken her to the grave spiritual consequences of her own actions and in an effort to prevent her from leading others into error, it was my responsibility to request that the governor refrain from receiving the Eucharist.

Unfortunately, a statement like that of Archbishop Naumann is the exception, not the rule. Patterns of behavior, ignored over time, become an institutional culture. When the Church fails to enforce her own standards, as a practical matter, those standards disappear. "If orders are consistently implemented to instruct the people, then the people will submit," writes Sun Tzu in his classic *The Art of War.* "If orders are not consistently implemented to instruct the people, then the people will not submit." The people of the

American Catholic Church have come to realize that their leaders in the hierarchy will not "implement orders"—will not enforce ecclesiastical laws—and consequently the people have come to ignore what the Church teaches.

Many bishops fear that if they take disciplinary action against a prominent Catholic public figure, their efforts will backfire, creating sympathy for the politician and gaining him votes. Quite likely they are right; viewed strictly from a political perspective, the move would probably backfire.

Similarly, parish priests fear that if they condemn artificial birth control in their Sunday homilies, they will foster resentment among their parishioners, the couples who use contraceptives will stop coming to Mass, their congregations will shrink, and thus they will lose opportunities to deliver at least some portion of the Gospel message. They are probably right too. If they did preach the message of *Humanae Vitae*, the priests' popularity would decline. Some of their parishioners would move to other parishes where the preaching was more congenial, while others might drift away from the practice of the Faith.

But even if the immediate consequences might be unpleasant, bishops and priests have a moral obligation to execute the laws of the Church faithfully and to preach the Gospel message in its fullness. A bishop should not be deterred from taking responsible disciplinary action because of the likely political fallout. A pastor should not withhold some portion of the Church's teaching, hiding a light under a bushel basket, because some parishioners might find the truth painful to accept. The role of the clergy is to teach, to govern, and to sanctify, not to calculate the political or economic consequences.

What would happen, after all, if the Church suffered a greater loss in popularity by preaching hard truths? Would that really be a loss, or might it be the first step on the road to revival? For most of a century, perceptive Catholic writers have been arguing that if Church leaders accepted the prospect of losing public respectability, they would, paradoxically, begin to regain it. Eighty years ago, in *Religion and the Modern State*, Christopher Dawson could foresee the crisis that was coming and was not afraid:

> Everywhere today the ruling forces in civilization seem converging against the Christian tradition. Modern civilization is not only ceasing to be Christian; it is setting itself up as an anti-religion which will tolerate no rival, and which claims to be sole master of the world. Never, perhaps, in the whole of its history has the People of God seemed weaker and more scattered, and more at the mercy of its enemies than it is today. Yet this is no reason for us to despair. The Christian law of progress is the very reverse of that of the world. When the Church possesses all the marks of external power and success, then is its hour of danger; and when it seems that no human power can save it, the time of its deliverance is at hand.

When Church leaders are clear and consistent in their statements and their actions—when they preach the Gospel in season and out of season, without worrying about their popularity ratings—their people rally around them. True, the parish congregations may shrink. True, many people who cannot accept the "hard saying" of the undiluted faith may desert the Church, just as many deserted Jesus when his preaching made them uncomfortable (see Jn 6:60–62). But those who remain will be firm in the Faith, and for those who fall away, the clear teaching of the Church will be a constant reminder, a prod to their consciences, spurring them toward reform.

On the other hand, when the teachings of the Church are muted, the bonds that hold together the Catholic community are not as tight. Thus, when Church leaders tone down their preaching, hoping to gain some political advantage by taking a subtle approach, they endanger the only real basis for their public leadership. Bishops have clout when they represent a strong, unified Catholic community. If the bonds of that community are eroded by confusion and dissent, the bishops' influence is undermined. So ironically, when Church leaders seek popular approval, in the long run they lose public influence. To regain that influence, they will have to set political considerations aside and concentrate on re-establishing their teaching authority. If that approach seems paradoxical, call it a leap of faith!

Ultimately a bishop's teaching authority rests on the common faith of the Catholic people. The faithful accept the bishop's leadership not because he puts forward convincing arguments (although he can and he should) but because they recognize him as a successor to the apostles, entrusted with the power of the Holy Spirit. The measure of his leadership on any issue, political or doctrinal, is the strength of his people's faith.

CHAPTER 8

The Cultural Revolution: The Enemy Without

Let us briefly return to February 1949 and again consider the words of Pope Pius XII in an address to a crowd in St. Peter's Square, at a time when Communist authorities were conducting the show trial of the heroic Hungarian Cardinal Mindszenty. Pope Pius XII asked his audience a question which we Catholics must answer today:

> Do you want a Church that remains silent when she should speak; that diminishes the law of God where she is called to proclaim it loudly, wanting to accommodate it to the will of man? Do you want a Church that departs from the unshakable foundations upon which Christ founded Her, taking the easy way of adapting Herself to the opinion of the day; a Church that is a prey to current trends; a Church that does not condemn the suppression of conscience and does not stand up for the just liberty of the people; a Church

that locks Herself up within the four walls of Her temple in unseemly sycophancy, forgetting the divine mission received from Christ: 'Go out the crossroads and preach the people'? Beloved sons and daughters! Spiritual heirs of numberless confessors and martyrs! Is this the Church you venerate and love? Would you recognize in such a Church the features of your Mother? Would you be able to imagine a Successor of St. Peter submitting to such demands?

Today many Catholics, indeed many Catholic prelates—including, sad to say, the sovereign pontiff—seem prepared to sue for peace with the secular culture. What sort of culture is it, and what sort of peace could be expected? Is it realistic to expect that the Faith could survive and flourish in a world dominated by what Pope John Paul II termed "the culture of death"?

A brief survey should suffice to demonstrate how far we as a country have fallen in.

We cannot read into the secret depths of human souls, so we cannot measure how much influence the Faith has on individuals. But we can observe how society has changed, especially regarding the issues that the Catholic Church considers most important. Since the family is the fundamental building block of any society, Catholic social teaching gives primary importance to the health and vigor of family life. So as we seek to discern the "signs of the times" and assess the strength of Catholic influence, we should begin with an appraisal of family life. Since I am an American, writing for a primarily American audience, let me focus on the

American family. What I say will, I am confident, apply to other societies in the Western world as well.

The outlook is bleak. In the course of my lifetime, America has experienced a spectacular breakdown in family life: an unprecedented disaster that threatens the future of our society. During the 1950s, the proportion of American marriages that ended in divorce hovered around 25 percent. Then in the 1960s, the number began a steady climb, and by the end of the 1970s, with the acceptance of "no-fault" divorce laws, reached toward 50 percent. The end of a marriage is not only a personal tragedy for the couple involved; the ripple effects reach out to their neighbors and their relatives. If there are children, those ripples are destructive waves. The breakdown of a family—or, in many cases, the absence of any functioning family from the outset—is not just *a* problem for children; it is *the* problem for children, dwarfing all other problems in its significance. Social scientists have shown, with one study after another, that children raised by their natural parents are more likely to be healthy, to perform well in school, to steer clear of crime and drug use and prison, to have successful careers, and to enter into stable marriages themselves. No other single indicator—not social or economic standing, nor family income, nor race nor religion nor education, nor even any combination of those things—comes close to matching the predictive value of this one factor: whether a child grew up with a mother and father at home.

To the troubling increase in the rate of divorce, add an equally troubling increase in the rate of out-of-wedlock births, which also deprive children of the advantages that come from being reared in a two-parent household. Today the rate of illegitimacy in the United States has soared to over 40 percent.

Young Americans today are less likely to marry than the members of their parents' generation, and less likely to stay married if they do finally tie the knot. They are also less likely to have large families, and Catholic couples are not much different from their neighbors in that respect. In the 1950s, the average American Catholic woman (excluding recent Hispanic immigrants) had 4.2 children; today that figure is 1.6 children: well below the replacement rate.

Without doubt, the main factor accounting for that sharp drop in fertility is the use of contraceptives. But another factor is the steady upward climb in the average age at which Americans enter into marriage. A woman who marries at the age of thirty, and then delays childbearing for a few more years while she establishes herself in a career, has already run through most of her fertile years. With the biological clock ticking, many couples who were once worried that they might have an unplanned pregnancy now begin worrying that they will *not* be able to achieve a pregnancy. So, perversely, the American generation that wanted to avoid children now sustains a large and lucrative industry offering "assisted reproduction." Women who used chemical and surgical means to disable their reproductive systems now rely on doctors to impregnate them.

Traditionally, medicine had been seen as a means of coping with the consequences of disease rather than coaxing human organs to do what they were not designed to do.

But then *in vitro* fertilization is not the first, nor the worst, widespread betrayal of the purposes of medicine.

Within thirty years after *Roe v. Wade*, the American legal system has not only enshrined abortion as an unassailable constitutional right but given unique privileges to abortion providers. Unlike grocery stores, gas stations, or savings banks, abortion clinics are given legal protection from peaceful demonstrations outside their doors.

At about the same time that the sexual revolution changed American moral behavior, another profound social change occurred: the suicide rate spiked. For generations, social scientists had tracked the incidence of suicide among young men, and over time the rate had remained remarkably steady. Then in the 1960s, the numbers suddenly jumped and settled in to remain at a new higher plateau. Was this further evidence of the "culture of death" denounced by Pope John Paul II? Was there a correlation between the breakdown of families and the self-inflicted deaths of men who might previously have realized their vocation as fathers? Social scientists have not answered—in fact they have not addressed—those questions. We do know, however, that by the end of the twentieth century there was growing pressure for legal acceptance of physician-assisted suicide.

Completing our tour through changes in public opinion on the issues that Pope John Paul II identified with the "culture of death," consider how far and how fast attitudes have changed toward homosexuality. In the middle of the twentieth century, a homosexual affair was still the "love that dare not speak its name," and as late as 2008, as a presidential candidate, Barack Obama opposed legal recognition of same-sex marriage. Now, barely a decade later, same-sex unions have gained that legal recognition, and anyone who objects is subject to the charge of "homophobia."

The gay-rights movement is in its own way more radical than the movement for legal abortion, and more directly inimical to Christian morality. Homosexual activists have not been content with the repeal of anti-sodomy laws; they demand that same-sex unions be recognized as legal marriages. In other words, they insist not only that they be allowed to conduct their affairs privately but even that society recognize those activities as a positive good, since marriage has always been recognized as an institution that benefits society.

With the legal recognition of same-sex marriage, our society took another decisive step away from its religious heritage. Christians, who recognize marriage as a permanent union between one man and one woman, were now required to affirm an impossibility: that two people of the same sex could be married. And within a few short years, the pressure was mounting for acceptance of another impossibility: that someone with male biological characteristics might be a female. Laws protecting the newfound rights of "transgendered" people were impinging on the rights of others, demanding that they affirm an untruth.

If opposition to homosexual unions is bigoted, it follows that it must be eliminated from polite society—by education first, then by lawsuits and other government action if necessary. Thus the schools, the courts, and the executive branch of the federal government have been enlisted in the fight to gain acceptance—and approval, remember!—for homosexuality.

Insofar as the Catholic Church defends the family based on marriage, the Church has now become a target for government enforcement of gay-friendly regulations. If bold Catholic bishops, priests, or lay people dare to give voice to the Church's teaching that homosexual actions are inherently disordered and morally wrong, they become even more prominent targets. Thus, the advance of the homosexual agenda threatens the religious freedom of American Catholics.

Already some Catholic institutions have collapsed in the face of the onslaught. In Massachusetts, Catholic charitable agencies stopped providing adoption services after they were instructed that they must provide equal treatment for same-sex couples, regardless of the Church's moral code. In San Francisco, the office of Catholic Charities complied by a similar mandate, until a Vatican directive forced the agency to stop handling adoptions directly; instead the Catholic office formed a pact with an independent agency that agreed to place children with homosexual couples. In Illinois, some Catholic adoption agencies closed down while others severed their formal diocesan affiliations. In each case—and more will surely follow—the Catholic agency was confronted with a direct challenge: it could only continue its ordinary business if it deserted its Catholic principles.

This is not another book about the decline of Western culture. In these last few pages I have merely been trying to provide a dramatic—and, by necessity, depressing—account of the enormous social changes we have observed in my lifetime. I do not pretend that this survey is scientific, because scientific precision is not necessary for my purposes. As Bob Dylan famously put it, "you don't need a weatherman to know which way the wind blows."

And that wind is still blowing. The social forces arrayed with the "culture of death" are still growing in strength; their plans are becoming steadily more ambitious. Rather than undermining the permanence of marriage (as they did by promoting "no-fault" divorce), now they aspire to change the very meaning of marriage. Not content with the legalization of surgical abortion on demand, they seek taxpayer subsidies for the procedure and over-the-counter distribution of abortifacient pills. (On that issue, too, the enemies of life aim to change the definition of terms, claiming that the deliberate destruction of an unborn human life is not an abortion if it takes place before the embryo is implanted in the mother's uterus.) Unsatisfied with public acceptance of homosexual acts, they now hope to have young schoolchildren instructed in how those acts are performed. Having overcome the resistance posed by defenders of traditional Christian moral principles, they now hope to ban the mention of those principles from public debate and even force believing Christians to betray their principles or face prosecution.

Compare the situation today with the America of the 1950s, when legal abortion was unthinkable, homosexuality was unmentionable, divorce was unrespectable, and illegitimate births unusual. How far our society has traveled in the course of a short lifetime! Now imagine what sort of society we might have fifty, or twenty, or even ten years from now if the collapse of family life continues and American culture continues to accelerate along the same unhappy path. Could our society survive?

The breakdown of public morality in America—and elsewhere in the Western world—was not unforeseen. Prudent Christians recognized, decades ago, that the trend of popular culture was profoundly adverse to the Faith. On a visit to the United States in 1976, the Polish Cardinal Karol Wojtyla predicted a dire confrontation between the Church and the forces of secular humanism:

> We are now standing in the face of the greatest historical confrontation humanity has gone through. I do not think that wide circles of American society or wide circles of the Christian community realize this fully. We are now facing the final confrontation between the Church and the anti-Church, of the Gospel versus the anti-Gospel.
>
> We must be prepared to undergo great trials in the not-too-distant future; trials that will require us to be ready to give up even our lives, and a total gift of self to Christ and for Christ. Through your prayers and mine, it is possible to alleviate this tribulation, but it is no longer possible to avert it. . . . How many times has the renewal of the Church been brought about in blood! It will not be different this time.

Unfortunately, while the future Pope John Paul II was calling for a revival of the "Church militant," most other Catholic leaders were making the case for accommodation with the popular culture. Rather than fighting to restore our society's moral compass, bishops used the prevailing cultural trends as an excuse to explain the flight from Catholic practice.

But a healthy Church—a healthy "cult"—should shape the culture, not be shaped by it. And if healthy Catholicism would form a healthy culture, at least among its own adherents, it would appear that Catholicism has not been healthy in these recent decades. Sure enough, over the same period that has seen the breakdown of American family life, the visible signs have shown a freefall in the profession and practice of the Catholic faith.

From 1965 to 2013, according to Georgetown University's Center for Applied Research in the Apostolate (CARA), the number of Catholic priests in the United States dropped by nearly one-third, from 58,632 to 39,600. The number of religious sisters plummeted by over 70 percent, from 179,954 to 51,247.

During that same time period, the country's Catholic population grew by somewhere between 45 and 60 percent, depending on which statistics one chooses. Consequently, there were far fewer priests ministering to far more parishioners. Kenneth Jones, in his *Index of Leading Catholic Indicators Since Vatican II*, reports that in 1965 there were 7.87 diocesan priests for every 10,000 American Catholics; by 2002, that figure was down to 4.6 priests per 10,000 faithful, and falling sharply. In 1965, only 3 percent of American Catholic parishes lacked a resident pastor; by 2002, that number had jumped to 15 percent and was growing, despite the decision to close parishes in many dioceses. In the 1960s, roughly one of every three Catholic children of grammar-school age attended a parochial school; by the 1990s, it was one in five, since Catholic schools, too, have been closing; that figure has skyrocketed in more recent years.

Some of those statistics undoubtedly reflect the unprecedented shock of the years following Vatican II—the years coinciding with cultural turmoil throughout the Western world—when thousands of priests and nuns left their rectories and convents, and tens of thousands of lay Catholics stopped going to church. But the downward spiral has continued into the twenty-first century. Looking at one diocese in the Midwest during the years 2000–2010—in a journal article with the provocative title "The Post-Christendom Sacramental Crisis"—theologian Ralph Martin found a 43 percent decrease in the number of infant baptisms, a 45 percent decrease in the number of Catholic marriages (along with an even larger 53 percent decrease in interfaith marriages), and a 15 percent decrease in the number of households registered in Catholic parishes.

The decline in religious life continues apace as well. Archbishop José Rodriguez Carballo, the secretary of the Vatican's Congregation for Religious, disclosed in October 2013 that about three thousand men and women leave religious life every year. The Society of Jesus, the religious order most closely identified with the formation of a strong Catholic cultural influence, has seen even greater attrition than the overall norm. On a worldwide basis, membership in the Jesuit order has dropped from 36,086 in 1966 to 17,676 in 2012. In the United States, the number of Jesuits, as of this writing, stands at 2,424, or 28 percent of its 1965 total.

The numbers tell only part of the story. Among those

Americans who do identify themselves as Catholics, most attend Mass only occasionally and go to confession rarely, if ever. In describing the situation as a "sacramental crisis," Ralph Martin explains, "The crisis consists in fewer and fewer baptized Catholics participating in the post-baptismal sacraments and fewer and fewer of the Catholics who do participate in further sacraments effectively realizing the fruits of these sacraments."

The negative trend reinforces itself. If parents go to Mass only occasionally, their children, absorbing the message that it is not a matter of importance, are likely to abandon the practice of the Faith altogether. One generation of inactive Catholics comes to church at Christmas and Easter; the next generation shows up only for weddings and funerals; the third generation sees no real point in having its children baptized.

Among those Americans who continue to identify themselves as Catholics, poll after poll proves that many dissent from the fundamental teachings of the Church, not only on political issues such as abortion and same-sex marriage, but also on essential dogmatic questions such as the Real Presence of Jesus in the Eucharist and the necessity of Christ's Sacrifice in the economy of salvation.

Since the advent of the automobile made "parish-shopping" practical, Catholics have had little difficulty in finding a community where they will be comfortable, regardless of their heterodox ideas. Some pastors are openly disdainful of Church teachings; others are afraid to raise controversial issues, fearful that their congregations will shrink even faster than they are shrinking already. In his book *The*

Decline and Fall of the Catholic Church in America, David Carlin foresees a pastoral disaster: "The churches that remain open on Sunday mornings will preach niceness to their few remaining members. But in the meantime, the religious vacuum in society will have created a moral vacuum, and who knows what monsters will rush in to fill those vacuums?"

The years of moral decadence in American public life have undeniably coincided with years of decline in the practice of the Catholic faith. Some might argue that the overall erosion in our culture *caused* the decline in Catholicism; I contend that the reverse is more nearly true. In any case, if we hope for Catholicism to exert a positive moral force upon our society, we must restore the active practice of the Catholic faith. We must address the internal problems of the Church before we can solve the troubles of society; we must revive the "cult" to repair the culture.

CHAPTER 9

The Limits of Tolerance:
The Enemy Within

"I see the Church as a field hospital after battle,"[36] Pope Francis said in a memorable interview with *America* magazine. He continued, "It is useless to ask a seriously injured person if he has high cholesterol and about the level of his blood sugars! You have to heal his wounds. Then we can talk about everything else. Heal the wounds, heal the wounds."

That striking image, to which the Holy Father has frequently returned, is undoubtedly an apt description of Christian charitable work. The faithful seek to heal wounds without necessarily asking how those wounds were inflicted.

But the field hospital exists to stabilize patients so that they can be sent along to another hospital, an institution with better equipment and a larger staff. And there the doctors *will* worry about their cholesterol and blood-sugar levels, and a host of other matters that did not seem urgent on the battlefield, because the objective is to return the patient to full health.

Or consider the image from a different perspective. A conscientious doctor treats patients to the best of his ability, regardless of how they contracted their illnesses. But if he is overwhelmed—if there are more patients than he can handle—eventually he begins asking questions about why so many people are unhealthy. It is striking, in fact, that in speaking of the Church as a field hospital, the pope is implicitly saying that our culture is a battlefield, where many are wounded and many of the wounds are self-inflicted.

At any hospital, even a field hospital, the doctor should certainly be aware of whether or not his work is succeeding, whether or not his patients are recovering. If there is rampant infection at the hospital, that problem must be addressed.

Finally, to measure the success of the field hospital, we must know what it means to be healthy. And that is precisely the problem that our society faces today: a breakdown in the understanding of what it means to be a healthy and complete human person. It is the mission of the Church in the twenty-first century, alongside her field-hospital work, to restore that understanding.

To recognize health implies recognition of disease, of what is not healthy. In spiritual terms, health means the avoidance of, or redemption and recovery from, sin. In the introduction to his magisterial *History of the Catholic Church*, James Hitchcock observes, "Even on a purely human level, history cannot be understood apart from the reality of sin, especially of universal selfishness. Rooted in universal human nature, sin is a constant in man's affairs, although its character and intensity vary from time to time. Those who deny that a tendency toward evil is basic to human nature cannot make sense of history, which becomes merely endless, incomprehensible tragedy."

To the modern secular mind, however, there is no such thing as sin. As Archbishop Fulton Sheen put it, "Everyone today is immaculately conceived. There are no penitents, only patients." Patients; we are back to the field hospital.

The denial of sin is not a twenty-first century development, to be sure. The great Cardinal John Henry Newman spotted the development and referred to it in a sermon in 1832: "What is the world's religion now? It has taken the brighter side of the Gospel, its tidings of comfort, its precepts of love; all darker, deeper views of man's condition and prospects being comparatively forgotten. This is the religion natural to a civilized age, and well has Satan dressed and completed it into an idol of the Truth."

The Church teaches the world about sin and salvation. The secular world hears only the latter part of the message and, lacking any consciousness of sin, cannot grasp the meaning of salvation. Thus is the message of the Gospel reduced to a gloss on the secular understanding of life: at best, the Golden Rule as a standard for a self-satisfied society; at worst, the sentimental bromides of Hallmark cards. When Christians accept the limitations of that outlook, they violate the injunction of St. Paul: "Do not be conformed to his world but be transformed by the renewal of your mind, that you may prove what is the will of God, what is good and acceptable and perfect" (Rom 12:2).

During his visit to the United States in 2008, Pope

Benedict XVI saw this problem as particularly acute in our society:

> Perhaps America's brand of secularism poses a particular problem: it allows for professing belief in God, and respects the public role of religion and the Churches, but at the same time it can subtly reduce religious belief to a lowest common denominator. Faith becomes a passive acceptance that certain things "out there" are true, but without practical relevance for everyday life. The result is a growing separation of faith from life: living "as if God did not exist." This is aggravated by an individualistic and eclectic approach to faith and religion: far from a Catholic approach to "thinking with the Church," each person believes he or she has a right to pick and choose, maintaining external social bonds but without an integral, interior conversion to the law of Christ. Consequently, rather than being transformed and renewed in mind, Christians are easily tempted to conform themselves to the spirit of this age.[37]

In past generations, the residue of old-fashioned Christian teaching about sin and salvation prevented the secular outlook from achieving a monopoly. But as the Church has gradually withdrawn from cultural conflicts, the secular approach has achieved a thorough dominance. Young people are instructed in the Christian faith, but all too often it is a denatured form of the Faith, which, like a weakened virus in a vaccine, serves to inoculate recipients against the stronger form.

When Pope John Paul II called for a "new evangelization" of the Western world, he knew that the project would be quite different from the original missionary work of introducing the Gospel message. That message had thoroughly penetrated Europe and the Americas, and was then gradually cast aside. Sophisticated modern men had developed a resistance to Christian thought.

J. Budziszewski explored the problem in a perceptive article that appeared in *First Things* in March 2014:

> The pagan wanted to be forgiven, but he did not know how to find absolution. To him the Gospel came as a message of release. But the neo-pagan does not want to hear that he needs to be forgiven, and so to him the Gospel comes as a message of guilt. . . . The pagan world was unfamiliar with Christian ideas. By contrast, the neo-pagan world is brimming with them. The makers of that world have even appropriated some of them—but have emptied them of Christian meaning.[38]

Budziszewski made one other poignant observation that deserves mention here, although it will be discussed at greater length later in this chapter: "In the ancient world, the people who needed to be evangelized were outside the walls of the Church; today they include thousands who are inside but who think just like those who are outside. When the Gospel is proclaimed, they complain."

An unapologetic defense of Catholic doctrine, particularly on the "hot-button" moral issues, is perceived as an affront to secularists. And, since most Catholics, including most priests and bishops, are averse to giving offense, we usually tend to avoid the questions that might strike exposed nerves. However, since these are exactly the questions that cause the gaping wounds in our society, our reticence means that we cannot function effectively as a field hospital, let alone as a teaching hospital.

Our society places an unusually high value on the virtue of tolerance of unorthodox ideas. Yet *is* tolerance a virtue? It is not a term found in the traditional taxonomy of virtues offered by Christian thinkers like St. Thomas Aquinas. If by "tolerance" we mean treating others with respect, even when we disagree with their views, then that is a virtue—although whether that virtue is properly characterized as "tolerance" is another question. But if it implies acceptance of evil, then tolerance is a vice.

In a brilliant book that has not received the attention it deserves, *The Long Truce*, A. J. Conyers argues that the modern commitment to tolerance deliberately blurs the difference between respecting other people and accepting their ideas. The elevation of tolerance to the ranking of a cardinal virtue in our society, he argues, stems from the implicit belief that if we could only set aside our petty differences over "little" things such as the search for absolute truth and the primacy of moral law, we would then all be better equipped to carry out the *real* business of building a powerful industrial state. In this context, Conyers believes, tolerance is a foundational virtue of the secular society since it presupposes that transcendent beliefs—the beliefs that form the "cult," which, in turn, forms the culture—are an unwelcome distraction from the purpose of our life together in a community.

That sort of "tolerance" is illustrated in the story of the Gadarene swine. Jesus rescued a man from demonic possession, a spectacular miracle and a great good for the community. In doing so, he sent the demons into a herd of pigs, which rushed into the sea and destroyed themselves, a great loss for the swineherds. The people could not understand how Jesus had worked this miracle, but they could understand that pigs were missing. They did not know who Jesus was, but they suspected that he was bad for business, and so "they began to beg Jesus to part from their neighborhood" (Mk 5:17).

The installation of tolerance as the ultimate social virtue, then, can lead very quickly to intolerance of the transcendent, to a desire to remove God from all public discussions, to look upon anyone who would raise religious questions as a danger to society. Paradoxically, in driving believers out of the marketplace of ideas, the champions of secularism claim that they are guarding society against intolerance, which, they imply, is inherent in the expression of any religious belief. The great twentieth-century Thomist Father Reginald Garrigou-Lagrange observed, "The Church is intolerant in principle because she believes; she is tolerant in practice because she loves. The enemies of the Church are tolerant in principle because they do not believe; they are intolerant in practice because they do not love."

In the United States, Catholicism struggled for generations to overcome far more blatant forms of intolerance. The first American colonies were settled by people who were avowed enemies of the religious establishment in England, and from the first days of the American republic, religious freedom was treated as an absolute necessity for a just society. But the willingness to respect diverse religious beliefs did not always extend to those of Roman Catholics, and overt hostility toward the Church, combined with hostility toward the waves of new immigrants, endured in public life well into the twentieth century.

America has always been a predominantly Christian country. But unlike the European nations from which we imported much of our cultural tradition, the United States has never been a Catholic country. The majority has always been Protestant, heirs of the Reformation and of the notion that every man must be free to choose his own faith. Consequently, although our foundational document refers to the founding of the country on "the laws of Nature and of Nature's God," in the American political tradition there is no assumption that the Church is the ultimate arbiter of God's laws. Our culture is (or was) Christian, but Christians sometimes disagree, and in America, an appeal to religious authority to resolve those disagreements was out of the question.

This quintessentially American willingness to set aside religious disagreements eventually enabled Catholics and Jews, Muslims and others to gain acceptance and become assimilated into society. But with assimilation came dangers. We want to be accepted by society but not to be absorbed. We want to maintain our own identity, distinctively American yet distinctively Catholic. We want to be able to influence society, not only to be influenced by society.

What does it tell the world, for instance, when a Catholic priest, invited to give a benediction at a public event, avoids mention of Jesus, or even God, in order to avoid giving offense to religious minorities? Yes, the prayer will be more "inclusive." But the priest represents the Catholic Church. Why would public officials bring in a Catholic priest to offer a blessing that could be given by anyone, lay or religious, Christian or not? What does it say when Pope Francis declines to give his apostolic blessing to a public audience, explaining that he knows some members of the audience are not believers? He thereby deprives the believing Catholics, who hoped to receive a papal blessing, and he confuses the non-believers, who must wonder whether the Catholic Church, which confers blessings on animals and on buildings, somehow thinks that a blessing cannot confer any benefit on non-Christians.

The Church exists to bring men to God, and as Cardinal Robert Sarah remarked in *God or Nothing*, "The most difficult thing for the postmodern world is to believe in God and in his only Son." So the "new evangelization" faces a formidable challenge. But to decline that challenge is to forsake the mission that Jesus entrusted to us. Cardinal Sarah warned, "If the tie between God and Christians is weakened, the Church becomes simply a human structure, one society among others. With that, the Church becomes trivial; she makes herself worldly and is corrupted to the point of losing her original nature. Indeed, without God we create a Church in our own image, for our little needs, likes, and dislikes. Fashion takes hold of the Church, and the illusion of sacredness become perishable, a sort of outdated medication."

Medication. There it is again, the image of the hospital. If the Church is to bring modern society back to health, it must administer the appropriate dose, sometimes of a medicine that society will find bitter. Loyalty to the Church entails a willingness to accept teachings that are not immediately congenial: teachings that do not readily fit with one's preferences. For conservative Catholics, that may mean an open attitude toward, and a willingness to learn from, Vatican statements on war and peace, on immigration policy, and on economic inequalities. For liberals, it will mean a recognition of the "non-negotiable" teachings regarding the dignity of life and the integrity of marriage. Loyal Catholics should have the humility to realize that they do not have all the right answers, and while the Church does not lay claim to political expertise, she does have special insights into "the laws of Nature and of Nature's God."

In every political discussion—whether the issue is abortion or marriage, war and peace or economics and welfare, capital punishment or immigration—the goal of the Church is not to impose sectarian policies but to awaken society to the demands of natural law. That goal is terribly important today in a society that is rapidly losing sight of natural law—and indeed of any notion of objective truth.

In a stunning passage from his opinion in the *Planned Parenthood v. Casey* case in 1992, Supreme Court Justice Anthony Kennedy provided a vivid example of secularist logic, writing, "At the heart of liberty is the right to define one's own concept of existence, of meaning, of the universe, and of the mystery of human life." If Justice Kennedy is to be taken seriously, liberty requires a completely subjective understanding of meaning, and a free society cannot admit any claims of objective truth. As Chicago's Cardinal Francis

George observed in his book *God in Action*, "Secularism captures the world for the profane, a realm from which God is banished."

Cardinal George draws a distinction between this perverse "secularism," which bars religious faith from public discussion, and a healthy "secularity" that allows for Church and state to function in their own proper spheres, with the government allowing full expression of religious beliefs and the Church recognizing the authority of the state in civil affairs, since the kingdom of God is not of this world. A healthy Church happily accepts a vigorous, independent secular government; secular politicians should be equally willing to recognize the benefits of a vigorous Church.

Militant secularists wish to draw an impenetrable wall between religious faith and public policy. Unfortunately, some Catholics are willing to accept that division, for either of two very different reasons. Some very conservative Catholics lean toward triumphalism, insisting that the government should obey the dictates of the Church, while other Catholics of more liberal inclinations believe that the Church should accommodate the demands of contemporary society.

The former group of Catholics insists that the Church holds a monopoly on truth in all spheres, and scoffs at the errors of the secular world. Rather than engaging in the political battle, these Catholics prefer to withdraw into their own enclaves from which they view the outside world with suspicion. For them, religious faith is a personal matter: a question of attaining their own salvation, devoid of any impulse to spread the Faith and enrich society with the message of the Gospel.

At the other extreme, the accommodationist impulse leads some Catholics to judge religious faith by the standards of the secular world. Thus, faith is seen as beneficial if it makes people feel good about themselves, or if it contributes to the overall welfare of society. David Carlin explained this willingness to accept the basic premises of secularism in his book *The Decline and Fall of the Catholic Church in America*: "The secularist agrees with *none* of the religious beliefs of the Christian; hence, everything the Christian believes becomes a matter of discomfort, when fraternizing with the secularist. . . . The easiest way of getting rid of this discomfort is either to discard these distinctively Christian beliefs or to soft-pedal them; and if this soft-pedal strategy is adopted over a long enough period, it becomes the practical equivalent of the discard strategy."

Both triumphalists and accommodationists are, in their own distinctive ways, cooperating with the secularists' ideas of Church-state separation. Both are subverting the public influence of the Church—not to mention the primary mission of the Church to spread the Gospel and baptize all nations. When the Church wholeheartedly pursues that divine mission, Catholic public influence will inevitably grow as a welcome by-product of effective evangelization. When the commitment to evangelization flags—as it will whenever either triumphalism or accommodationism holds sway—society is deprived of an effective Christian public witness, while the Church is deprived of new converts.

The notion that the Church should accept a "wall of separation" between Church and State, between faith and reason, is a tenet of the philosophical approach which Catholic theologians once identified as Modernism, and which the First Vatican Council roundly condemned. In his encyclical *Pascendi Dominici Gregis* in 1907—just more than one hundred years ago, not a long stretch of time by the standards of an institution that routinely measures its history in centuries—Pope Pius X wrote that the Modernists were "the most pernicious of all the adversaries of the Church" because of "their designs for her undoing, not from without but from within."[39]

Was Pius X, a canonized saint, entirely wrong about Modernism? Was the First Vatican Council wrong to denounce the trend? If a Roman pontiff and an ecumenical council could be wrong a century ago, how can Catholics be confident that another pope and another ecumenical council are right today? Yet that is precisely the message that Cardinal Oscar Maradiaga delivered to an audience in Dallas in 2013. The Honduran cardinal, the chairman of the pope's top advisory board, said that the Second Vatican Council had been convened to "end the hostilities between the Church and Modernism, which was condemned in the First Vatican Council." Lest anyone miss the message, he added, "Modernism was, most of the time, a reaction against injustices and abuses that disparaged the dignity and the rights of the person."

Notice here that Cardinal Maradiaga was not saying that *some* aspects of Modernism could be reconciled with Catholic teaching; he was not saying that Modernism might have been misunderstood. On the contrary, he was saying that Modernism was opposed to "injustices and abuses"—undoubted evils—even as he reminded his audience that the

Church had condemned Modernism a century ago. Does the logic of his address not suggest that, at the First Vatican Council, the Church had sided with injustices and abuses? Did his highly publicized speech not play into the hands of those who saw the Second Vatican Council as a dramatic break with—if not an outright repudiation of—past Church teachings?

Vatican I warned the faithful that Modernism is incompatible with Catholic doctrine. According to Cardinal Maradiaga, Vatican II taught that Modernism is compatible with Catholic doctrine, and indeed might be a more authentic form of Catholicism. In the absence of clear distinctions and explanations—which the Honduran cardinal did not offer to his audience in Dallas—these two expressions of Catholic teaching are incompatible. How can they be resolved?

One very attractive option, unfortunately, lies in the familiar tendency, now deeply ingrained in the instincts of the Catholic hierarchy, to ignore the problem. Indeed it could be said that the habit of denial, the tendency on the part of the hierarchy to downplay difficulties and attempt to avoid problems, has become something close to an established policy in the Church since Vatican II.

A Case Study: The Betrayal of Chinese Catholics

In my recent book *Lost Shepherd*, I advanced the argument that Pope Francis has systematically undermined the established doctrines and disciplines of the Catholic Church, not by officially denying or rescinding them, but by encouraging Church leaders to ignore them, to act as if they did not exist.

I will not rehash that argument here; I invite readers to see that previous book. Instead let me examine just one clear example of the pope's method, which was announced just as I finished working on this book.

On September 22, the Vatican announced the signing of an agreement with the government of China giving the Beijing regime a role in the appointment of new Catholic bishops. Although the terms of the accord were not made public, informed sources at the Vatican confirmed that under the agreement, the Beijing government would name candidates for episcopal office, with the pope allowed a choice from among those recommended for the posts.

In a statement explaining the accord, Cardinal Pietro Parolin, the Secretary of State, emphasized that "the objective of the Holy See is a pastoral one: the Holy See intends just to create the condition, or help to create the condition, of a greater freedom, autonomy, an organization"[40] for the Catholic Church in China.

The pact was the long-awaited response to a very real pastoral problem: the Catholic Church in China had long been divided between the "official" Church, sanctioned by the regime, and the "underground" Church, fiercely loyal to the Holy See. Although the distinctions were blurred—many "official" bishops had quietly sought and received the approval of the Vatican—the "underground" Church was still unrecognized, and frequently harassed, by civil authorities. Proponents of the new accord argued that it would ease restrictions on the Church and heal divisions.

Opponents of the deal disagree, reasoning that by giving greater power to the Beijing government, the agreement would ultimately increase the pressure on the "underground" Church. Cardinal Joseph Zen, the retired bishop of Hong Kong and implacable opponent of the Communist government, said angrily that Cardinal Parolin should resign because of his "betrayal" of China's faithful Catholics.

In his own statement, Cardinal Parolin observed that the accord could bring unity to the Chinese Church. He reasoned, "For the first time in decades, today all the bishops in China are in communion with the Bishop of Rome." That was true, but only because in making the deal, Pope Francis agreed to lift the excommunications incurred by Chinese bishops who had been installed by the Beijing regime in defiance of the Holy See. Also, as part of the accord, the Vatican persuaded two "underground" bishops—prelates who, like all leaders of the underground Church, had paid a heavy price for their loyalty to the Vatican, being subject to police harassment and the prospect of arbitrary arrest—to resign and be replaced by government-approved bishops.

In 2007, in a letter to the Church in China, Pope Benedict XVI said that the Catholic Patriotic Association, a body set up by the Communist regime to control the Church, could never play a legitimate role in the structure of the Church. In 2018, in signing the accord with Beijing, the Vatican allowed for the Patriotic Association, and companion groups set up by the regime, to put forward candidates to become diocesan bishops. Defenders of the pact emphasized that the pope would make the final selection of bishops. But his selection would be made from among the favored candidates chosen by Chinese authorities: the same authorities who continued to advance an official ideology that denounced religious faith.

In October 2018, as prelates from around the world gathered in Rome for the Synod of Bishops, Pope Francis announced, with tears in his eyes, that for the first time two prelates from mainland China had been allowed to join in a meeting of the universal Church. But it was noteworthy that the two Chinese bishops were also ranking officials in organizations approved by the government. Other Chinese Catholic bishops, not leaders of "official" organizations, were still not at liberty to travel to Rome.

"There are no automatic guarantees that the quality of Chinese Catholic religious life will improve,"[41] wrote Father Antonio Spadaro, an enthusiastic supporter of the pact, in *Civilta Cattolica*. He admitted that the agreement would face challenges, notably including "the challenge of Siniciza-tion"—that is, the regime's insistence that every institution in China must promote the national ideology.

Nevertheless, Father Spadaro predicted that the agreement would reap great pastoral benefits. To explain the reasoning behind the Vatican's willingness to sign the pact, he cited with approval the thoughts expressed by Pope Francis: "For me, China has always been a reference point of greatness. A great country. But more than a country, a great culture, with unending wisdom. As a boy, whatever I read about China would fill me with admiration. I admired China. Later, I studied the life of Matteo Ricci and I say that he felt the same thing I felt: admiration. I understood how he was able to dialogue with this great culture and its ancient wisdom. He was able to meet it.

A great culture, yes. Ancient wisdom, yes. And also, might I add, from a pastoral perspective, more than one billion souls in need of salvation, more than one billion people to whom we might preach the Gospel, to whom the Church might bring the fundamental message of sin and salvation. That is, the Church could bring that message if she were allowed to preach the Gospel. Despite the Vatican-Beijing agreement, there was no sign that the Chinese regime would relax in its drive to banish religious faith, to rule that preachers cannot use the airwaves, that believers cannot hold public office, that police may break up "unauthorized" household prayer services, that anyone who is truly in harmony with the spirit of China (see "Sinicization") would be expected to eschew religious ties.

The bulk of Father Spadaro's *Civilta Cattolica* essay was devoted to a historical survey of Church agreements with various government regimes. He remarked, "The history of the Church [with respect to episcopal appointments] is rather to be considered as the history of the search for agreements with political authorities on the nomination of bishops." He cited, for example, the 1801 concordat with Napoleon, which helped the Church in France recover from the disastrous effects of the French Revolution. But whatever the benefits of the concordat with Napoleon, it was wrought more than two centuries ago. During that time, the Church has battled for freedom from government interference—at considerable cost, but also with considerable success. A move *back* to the standard of Church-state relations that prevailed in 1801 can only be seen as a setback for the Catholic cause.

Even after concluding the secret agreement with the

Vatican, Chinese authorities have refused to recognize the "underground" Church. An online directory of Chinese Catholic institutions released by government-approved editors immediately after the accord did not include any priests or parishes of the "underground" Church. In the quest to normalize relations with an avowedly atheistic regime, the Vatican had betrayed the trust of the very Chinese Catholics who had sacrificed the most for their loyalty to Rome.

A Crisis of Leadership

The hierarchical Church, the Petrine Church, is always tempted to form alliances with worldly powers. But in the early twenty-first century, yielding to that temptation involves a deadly irony, because the world's secular powers are collapsing.

The fall of the Soviet empire was a vivid recent reminder that no regime—no matter how powerful, no matter how brutal—can long survive if it violates the essential promptings of human nature. Today the dominant culture in the Western world, a culture of secular materialism and individualism, is tottering under the weight of its own errors because it suppresses the essential truths of man's spiritual nature, his quest for God, his longing for redemption.

The world today cries out for the truths of the Gospel. Too often, sadly, the institutional Church, deformed by the habits of denying obvious problems and withholding hard truths, does not respond. If our Church leaders are not serving our world with the fullness of the Gospel, then it falls to

169

faithful lay Catholics to *demand* the truth from their pastors, not just the truth about the corruption that has blighted the Church (although that will be a necessary first step), but the whole truth about the human condition.

"Who is going to save our Church?" asked Archbishop Sheen. "Do not look to the priests. Do not look to the bishops. It's up to you, the laity, to remind our priests to be priests and our bishops to be bishops." If the dismal summer of 2018 is to produce any good result, it will be by underlining that message. The loyal Catholic laity, stirred by anger into action, will demand an end to the corruption of the Church and a full return to her evangelical purpose.

At the turn of the seventh century, Pope Gregory the Great spoke in a homily about a failing of bishops that "discourages me greatly." Accusing himself of the same weakness that he saw among his brother bishops, he said, "We abandon the ministry of preaching and, in my opinion, are called bishops to our detriment, for we retain the honorable office but fail to practice the virtues proper to it. Those who have been entrusted to us abandon God, and we are silent. They fall into sin, and we do not extend a hand of rebuke. . . . We are wrapped up in worldly concerns, and the more we devote ourselves to external things, the more insensitive we become in spirit."

The mistaken belief that bishops always have the power to speak on behalf of "the Church" plays into the popular misconception that bishops could, if they wished, change unpopular Catholic doctrines. The perception of the Church as a multinational corporation, with bishops (and ultimately the pope) wielding executive control, encourages secular critics to argue that the hierarchy should tailor dogmas to match popular styles. Even the notion that doctrines should be established by public opinion reflects the clericalist mentality. It derives from the assumption that the Church is our possession, operating under our guidance.

The truth, which bears constant repetition, is that the Church belongs to Christ and is guided by the Holy Spirit. Bishops are not executives for a corporate enterprise; they are fathers to a large spiritual family. The Roman pontiff himself does not have the authority to alter the teachings of the Church. He can sometimes speak with great authority, but only within the constraints of established doctrine, in line with tradition, under the guidance of the Holy Spirit. In an important sense, the pope has far *less* freedom to promote his own opinions than ordinary people like you and me. He speaks with authority only when he does not speak for himself, and he commands only in his role as "the servant of the servants of God."

When bishops fall into the error of thinking of themselves as branch managers of an international enterprise, they soon develop unhealthy habits. They look to the national bishops' conference for guidance on important issues rather than taking initiative themselves—and thereby reinforce the mistaken public perception that the episcopal conference has more authority than the individual bishop. They pass off responsibility for unpopular Church teachings, saying that they are following the policies set by the Vatican, rather than taking their proper responsibility as teachers and explaining those teachings. When he says that he is looking forward to the decentralization of Church leadership, Pope Francis surely means that he hopes to root out these errors and make bishops clearly responsible for teaching, preaching, and setting policies in their own dioceses.

Along with their bishops, pastors and priests and religious who administer Catholic schools and hospitals can also fall into the trap of picturing themselves as the proprietors of the Church. In her book *The Long Loneliness*, Dorothy Day spoke of the "scandal of businesslike priests"—the grave spiritual damage done by busy clerics who pride themselves on handling the details of parish administration, giving short shrift to the welfare of the souls entrusted to their care.

Under ordinary circumstances, the owner of a piece of property has the power not only to manage that property but also to divest himself of it, to sell off all or part of his estate when he finds it convenient. Church officials may have the same sort of power as a matter of secular law; the bishop, for instance, is the legal executive of the secular corporation that holds diocesan assets. But a bishop, a religious superior, or the chief officer of a Church-administered hospital does not own the assets; he holds them in trust, to be managed for the good of the faithful.

Still, because there are few meaningful restrictions on a bishop's legal authority over diocesan assets, bishops can and sometimes do misuse the resources that have been entrusted to their care. In the years before the sex-abuse scandal came to light, bishops routinely paid large settlements to the victims of priests' predation, insisting that the cases must remain undisclosed. When the abuse came to light, bishops authorized additional payments of millions to victims as well as millions to the diocesan lawyers who contested the victims' claims. In all those cases, there was precious little consultation with the laity, with the people who had donated the funds that were being so rapidly dissipated. When the frightening costs of the scandal forced the closing of Catholic parishes and parochial schools, again bishops made their own decisions about which parishes and schools would be eliminated, rarely providing opportunities for lay people—the parishioners and the parents of students in those schools—to participate in the decision-making process.

More ominously, several bishops, in order to avoid prosecution for their endangering children and for failing to report crimes, entered into plea-bargaining agreements with local prosecutors. In a few cases, these agreements imposed obligations not only on the bishops themselves but on their successors; their dioceses were required to submit reports to, and clear policies with, local public officials. In other words, these bishops yielded up the religious freedom of the Church to preserve their own personal freedom. The deals they struck might be described as photographic negatives of martyrdom as, rather than laying down their own lives for the sake of others, too many of our bishops surrendered the patrimony of generations of Catholics to protect themselves. That has been one way in which bishops have betrayed the faithful in recent years.

Yet there is another way of betrayal, more insidious for its negative consequence for the souls of those same faithful. Clergy, whether bishops or priests, who regard themselves as the proprietors of the Church may be tempted to "give away" the moral teachings of Catholicism. If he thinks of himself as the sole arbiter of what constitutes the true

Faith, a priest may tell his parishioners that they need not worry about belief in the Real Presence, or about a divorce and remarriage, or about a bit of false testimony in a court case. If the pastor operates on the belief that he "owns" the Church, he can make his own rules. If he makes his own rules, his parishioners will be all the more likely to lapse into the same error, believing that they can be justified by the unilateral decision of their priest rather than by the universal sacrifice of Christ.

In the first volume of his work *Theo-Drama*, the theologian Hans Urs von Balthasar wrote about the false unity within the Church, which "consists of people who, if they are officeholders, are inclined to change their office from a *ministerium* to a *dominium*; if they are laypeople, they tend to dwell on their maturity over against the officeholders." In this way, he observed, "The uniqueness of unity in Christ collapses, and in its place arises the unities fabricated by men, robbing the Church (or the fragments of her that remain) of her credibility, lacking any note of her essential mystery."

The temptation to seize power for oneself—to convert a *ministerium* into a *dominium*—is a natural human weakness closely linked to the will for power. In the powerful parable of the vineyard (Mt 21:33–43), Jesus tells of the workers who, when they see the owner's son, say, "Let us kill him and have his inheritance." Church workers are rarely so blunt in their aspirations for power, but the same urge is at work: the urge to seize control, to be rid of a master, to say *non serviam*.

Over the course of centuries, many ecclesiastical leaders have been tempted to seize power not only in the Church but in the political world as well. It is instructive to observe the net results of their Machiavellian maneuvers. Popes and prelates have gained control over duchies and provinces and countries, but they have never managed to hold power. The "papal states" have shriveled into a tiny sovereign plot, completely surrounded by secular Rome. Personally, I have sometimes questioned, not entirely in jest, whether it's possible that, as the price for their power to speak authoritatively on matters of faith and morals, Catholic prelates are saddled with a sort of reverse infallibility—an inability ever to make the right judgment—on questions of practical politics.

Prescinding from the great questions of power politics, however, consider how the same will to power is made manifest on the local scale, by ordinary bishops and pastors, in the desire for comfort and prestige. Pastors have cooks and secretaries to help them with their work. The parish school might close, but the sumptuous rectory remains, with one or two priests comfortably ensconced in a building designed to accommodate five or six men. Bishops are surrounded by their staff aides, protected from untoward meetings with unhappy members of their flocks. St. John Neumann, who was Archbishop of Philadelphia from 1852 to 1860, once walked twenty-five miles in a day to confirm a single young man. Today, American bishops, who have cars and drivers at their disposal, schedule confirmations only once every two or three years for each parish cluster.

Am I making sweeping, unfair generalizations? Yes. Some bishops and priests work themselves to exhaustion. I am personally familiar with pastors who never take vacations, who devote every waking hour to their flocks. Yet I am also familiar with priests who live a life of ease, putting in only a few hours of work each week. When the natural human temptation toward idleness sets in, there are very few restraints on a priest who views himself as an independent contractor. If he celebrates Mass on Sunday and the parish bills are paid, he can probably escape criticism for his long weekends, his weekday golf outings, his long evenings in front of the television with a drink in his hand.

Conscientious priests work steadily, while idle priests waste their time. But virtually all priests, good or bad, defend the rights and privileges of the clergy. Still more determinedly, all bishops defend the prestige of the hierarchy. The powerful impulse toward clerical solidarity—as if priests were members of a labor union—wreaked havoc on the American Church when bishops were caught defending predatory priests. But the same impulse still protects lazy priests, dissident priests, self-indulgent priests.

Pastors (and again, especially bishops) have also learned that they can demand respect and obedience from loyal Catholics, even when dissident Catholics and critics of the Church berate them. Bishops who have shown extraordinary restraint in their dealings with rebellious nuns or heretical theologians are quick to slap down orthodox Catholics who raise their voices against abuses within the Church. Radical Catholics may be free to denounce Church teachings, but conservative laymen are expected to swallow their complaints and show their fidelity. Like schoolyard bullies, some prelates pick their fights carefully, choosing opponents who will not fight back. In *Anglican Difficulties*, John Henry Newman wrote of a hierarchy whose members "are wont to shrink from the contumacious, and to be valiant towards the submissive." He did not escape that phenomenon when he entered the Catholic Church.

In an insightful Erasmus Lecture in 2013, Rabbi Jonathan Sacks, who was Chief Rabbi of the Hebrew Congregations of the Commonwealth from 1993 to 2013, observed that the prophet Jeremiah, addressing his captive nation living in exile in Babylon, taught the people of Israel to see themselves as set apart from the concourse of nations, from the political world. The Chosen People betrayed their mission, the prophet said, when they saw their success or failure exclusively in political terms. Rabbi Sacks said:

> The Israelites had betrayed their mission by becoming obsessed with politics at the cost of moral and spiritual integrity. So taught all the prophets from Moses to Malachi. Every time you try to be like your neighbors, they said, you will be defeated by your neighbors. Every time you worship power, you will be defeated by power. Every time you seek to dominate, you will be dominated. For you, says God, are my witnesses to the world that there is nothing sacred about power or holy about empires and imperialism.

The People of God, in the Old Testament and the New, stand apart from the world as a reminder that political success and economic achievement are not the ultimate purposes of human life. There is something more important than the marketplace, more important than the state. If religious bodies do not issue that reminder, the people are prone to forget, and the power of the imperial state grows.

What the Faithful Laity Can Do

Hope in the Form of a Creative Minority

Rabbi Sacks made that observation in a discussion of the notion of a "creative minority"—a concept that then-Cardinal Ratzinger had popularized before his election as Peter's successor. The German cardinal had advanced the thesis that the Church is most effective when her people act as a creative minority in society, not achieving authority over society, but acting as a restraint on those who govern and pricking the consciences of those in power. The Church of the early twenty-first century, visibly losing prestige and influence, was probably destined to become a creative minority once again, Cardinal Ratzinger said. *In Faith and the Future,* he wrote:

> From the crisis of today the Church of tomorrow will emerge—a Church that has lost much. She will become small and will have to start afresh more or less from the beginning. She will no longer be able to inhabit many of the edifices she built in prosperity. As the number of her adherents diminishes, so will she lose many of her social privileges. In contrast to an earlier age, she will be seen much more as a voluntary society, entered only by free decision.

This smaller Church would no longer feel the siren call of human respect. Indeed, the creative minority would emerge because of a willingness to flout the standards of a secular society. Belonging to this Church would mean forfeiting any hope of social climbing; it would mean a life of skirmishing against convention. "As a small society," Cardinal Ratzinger said, the Church "will make much bigger demands on the initiative of her individual members."

When he described his vision of the Church as a creative minority, Cardinal Ratzinger was not overly sanguine about the practical consequences for the faithful. The Church would be poor, the Faith would be disdained, and the faithful would suffer, he predicted. In this way, however, the Church would be better conformed to Jesus Christ. Thus he concluded, "But when the trial of this sifting is past, a great power will flow from a more spiritualized and simplified Church."

For decades now, faithful Catholics, hoping for signs of a genuine revival in the American Church, have looked anxiously to the traditional indices of Catholic vitality: the rate of attendance at Sunday Mass, the number of young people entering the priesthood or religious life, the openings of new parishes and parochial schools. By those standard measurements, the decline of American Catholicism, which began in the 1960s and accelerated through the 1970s, is still continuing.

There are a few hints that the rate of decline may be slowing: an uptick in the number of young men entering the seminaries in some dioceses, the steady expansion of certain religious orders. But the onslaught of negative stories—the parishes and schools closed—drowns out the good news.

Still, statistics never tell the whole story, especially about a subject like religious faith. Are those standard measurements the wrong way to assess the vigor of Catholic life? Is it possible that a new Catholic renaissance has already begun, passing undetected because it arises in unexpected places, by unexpected means?

In more than thirty years as a journalist covering Catholicism, I have found that the most exciting signs of vigorous life in the Church often (I am tempted to say always) come from unexpected directions. Official renewal programs, launched by diocesan committees under the guidance of expensive consultants, begin with great fanfare but end with meager results. Meanwhile, far from the limelight, prayerful Catholic individuals, without formal credentials and without financial support, working alone or in small groups, quietly work wonders.

My favorite example of this phenomenon—and arguably the greatest success story of twentieth-century American Catholicism—is the growth of the Eternal Word Television Network (EWTN). Who could have predicted that a cloistered nun with no background whatsoever in broadcasting, and with debilitating physical ailments, could found a Catholic radio-television empire that would span the globe? Mother Angelica began with nothing but a vision and a commitment supported by faith. She had no experience or expertise in broadcasting, no connections with the industry, no powerful corporate sponsors. She was, by the world's ordinary standards, completely unqualified for the work she chose to undertake. For years, she faced opposition from the US bishops' conference, which poured millions of dollars into a competitive effort. Yet against all odds it was EWTN that prospered, while the lavishly funded effort by the bishops' conference disappeared from the scene without leaving a trace.

The moral of the story is that the movements of the Holy Spirit cannot be confined within the guidelines set by diocesan committees and episcopal conferences. "The wind blows where it wills, and you hear the sound of it, but you do not know whence it comes or whither it goes; so it is with everyone who is born of the Spirit" (Jn 3:8).

The Second Vatican Council boldly proclaimed that we are living in "the age of the laity." (Immediately after the council, thousands of priests and religious rushed out to take posts in the secular world, doing the work of the laity, and leaving lay men and women to run the parishes and schools they were neglecting, in a thorough inversion of the council's message. But that is another story.) If the Holy Spirit was speaking through the council fathers, then it should come as no surprise that the most conspicuous signs of growth in Catholicism since that time have come through the movements founded by and/or dedicated to the laity: the charismatic renewal, Opus Dei, the pro-life movement, Cursillo, Focolare, L'Arche, the NeoCatechumenal Way, and many more. The growth of these movements has been uneven, marked by occasional missteps and some serious wrong turns. But the *vigor* of the movements is undeniable. Pope John Paul II referred to the movements as "the finger of the Holy Spirit on the Church."

And keep in mind that a revival in the Church does not necessarily appear as a "movement," as an institution or organization that will be listed in a diocesan directory. The revival could be ignited by small groups of people who come together to pray, to study the Scriptures, or to read the classics of Catholic spirituality. Or it may be parents who make the decision to homeschool their children. Or it may be lay people who take the initiative to organize Eucharistic Adoration in their parishes. All these things are happening today, far more often than most Catholics realize, without attracting public attention.

Many good Catholics will read these words and wonder whether I am missing the larger picture. There may be pockets of growth in the Catholic Church, they will concede, but the world around us is growing steadily more hostile to the Faith—indeed, to any faith. Our society is rushing headlong toward a new kind of paganism, pushing religious beliefs ever further toward the periphery of public consciousness. And the abuse scandal has done incalculable damage to the authority of the teaching Church. I would concede the point. But it does not change my argument.

Catholicism has always shown the greatest vigor under adverse conditions. As our society drifts further from its Christian moorings, believers become more aware of the need for apostolic courage and vigor. Vladimir Lenin, who knew a thing or two about revolution, urged his Bolshevik followers to "heighten the contradictions," to present people with a clear choice. Today the contradictions between a Christian faith and a secular culture are becoming clearer by the day, and serious Christians are faced with a serious choice: to make their peace with a decadent society or to take a countercultural stand. When Christians make that choice— and *only* when they make it—they become a powerful force capable of transforming a society. From the perspective of the Faith, then, the key question is not whether secular culture is growing more perverse—it is—but whether Catholics are becoming more likely to resist that unhappy trend.

So let me ask the question again. Could there be something stirring within the Church: a subterranean rumbling, a movement for renewal that could burst forth to change the religious landscape? I am confident the answer to that question is yes.

"Christians are born for combat," Pope Leo XIII wrote. It is the nature of a faithful Catholic, he explained, to follow Christ by espousing unpopular ideas and by defending the truth, even at great personal cost: "To recoil before an enemy, or to keep silence when from all sides such clamors are raised against truth, is the part of a man either devoid of character or who entertains doubt as to the truth of what he professes to believe. The only ones who win when Christians stay quiet are the enemies of truth. The silence of Catholics is particularly disturbing because frequently a few bold words would have vanquished the false ideas."[42]

So any aspiring Catholic reformer, and that includes bishops and priests, must ask himself: am I willing to pay the price? Or rather: How much am I ready and able to pay? A question, no doubt, best asked in prayer. The posture of being on one's knees in front of a crucifix tends to clarify one's thoughts.

Live Not By Lies

Just before he was exiled from the Soviet Union in 1974, the great Russian writer Aleksandr Solzhenitsyn wrote a challenging essay entitled "Live Not By Lies."[43] (The essay was reprinted in translation by the *Washington Post* on January 18, 1974, and again after Solzhenitsyn's death, on August 5, 2008.) In that essay, he outlined a strategy for bringing down the tyrannical Soviet regime. The same strategy—a refusal to tolerate falsehood—could also break the stranglehold of secularism and allow the revival of Christian culture.

Solzhenitsyn asked reformers to adhere to a simple rule: refuse to accept lies; refuse to participate in lies. "Though lies conceal everything, though lies embrace everything, we will be obstinate in this smallest of matters," he wrote. "Let them embrace everything, but not with any help from me."

The Russian author recognized that not every Russian would be ready to make the same commitments, and not everyone would find himself in the same position to effect change. The costs of reform, he warned, would be spread unevenly: "No, it will not be the same for everybody at first. Some, at first, will lose their jobs. For young people who want to live with truth, this will, in the beginning, complicate their young lives very much, because the required recitations are stuffed with lies, and it is necessary to make a choice."

Solzhenitsyn was a prophet, not only in the sense that he spoke the truth, but also in that he correctly identified the force that could, and eventually did, bring down the powerful Soviet empire. "Live Not by Lies" was written at a time when the power of the Communist police state was still unquestioned. (In fact, Solzhenitsyn was arrested by the KGB on the very day that he completed the essay.) Even then—long before most of us had ever heard of the Solidarity movement, or learned to recognize the name "Wojtyla," long before Reagan challenged Gorbachev to "tear down this wall"—Solzhenitsyn recognized that a corrupt and tyrannical regime cannot endure if ordinary people simply refuse to recognize its legitimacy.

The fearsome Soviet regime, which once threatened to take over the entire world, finally collapsed because it was built upon a friable foundation. Prudent Western leaders and fierce Afghan rebels played their roles, but they were only supporting actors. Ultimately Communism fell because the public no longer believed—or even pretended to believe—an ideology of lies. For decades, this evil form of government had survived and flourished through the systematic use of violence. But in the long run, violence is no substitute for honest legitimacy. Solzhenitsyn saw it clearly in 1974: "But violence quickly grows old. And it has lost confidence in itself, and in order to maintain a respectable face it summons falsehood as its ally—since violence can conceal itself with nothing except lies, and the lies can be maintained only by violence. And violence lays its ponderous paw not every day and not on every shoulder. It demands from us only obedience to lies and daily participation in lies—all loyalty lies in that."

Not every Russian had the courage of Solzhenitsyn; not many were willing to risk imprisonment in the Gulag Archipelago. But this anti-Communist prophet saw that there was a milder form of effective resistance: "Let us refuse to say that which we do not think." To counteract the power of lies, he said, "Our path is not to give conscious support to lies about anything whatsoever!"

A decade after Solzhenitsyn wrote those words, the Solidarity movement—refusing to honor the lie that a Communist regime represented the interests of the working class—had exposed the weakness of the Polish government. The epidemic of honesty spread quickly, and within another decade, the Soviet Union was no more.

In their obituary notices on the Russian writer, Western eulogists have generally acknowledged Solzhenitsyn as the foremost critic of Soviet ideology. They have been less willing to recognize the force of his critique of Western consumerism. But there are lies at the heart of secular materialism too, as Popes John Paul II and Benedict XVI have often warned us. Solzhenitsyn's unforgettable Harvard commencement address also merits a fresh reading, twenty-five years after it was delivered.

For now, however, I want to focus on the simple moral strategy suggested in "Live Not by Lies." It is a sound strategy, which can be used to combat any sort of corruption in places of authority—even within our Church. The Catholic Church has very little in common with the Soviet Union, of course. Yet any offense against truth is an offense against the Faith, and so the virtue of honesty has a cleansing effect within the Church.

Solzhenitsyn reminds his fellow Russians that in order to bring about change, they do not necessarily need to be heroes or revolutionaries. He asks them to set a more modest standard, reckon how far their circumstances allow them to join in the quiet revolution, and then, within those personal parameters, refuse to participate in spreading lies. An honest man, he said, having committed himself to that standard,

"Will not henceforth write, sign, or print in any way a single phrase which in his opinion distorts the truth." He goes on to suggest the meetings that one should not attend, the committees that one should not join, the publications to which one should not subscribe.

Imagine how much change would be wrought if ordinary Catholics would adopt the same standard. Below I have suggested some of the steps that concerned lay Catholics might take, and some of the mistakes that we should avoid—a list of dos and don'ts—to promote candor and honesty, and thus to advance the cause of reform within the Church.

We cannot right every wrong. We cannot expect instantaneous change. We are not, most of us, in a position to effect positive changes within ecclesiastical institutions. Yet we can all promote reform within the Church simply by recognizing forthrightly that some reform is necessary.

We may not all be crusaders. We may not all be heroes. But we all can recognize and honor the truth. We all can reject the lies, and we can all, yes all of us, strive to be saints.

What Every Lay Catholic Should—and Should Not—Do

DO

- Pray for the universal Church, and for your diocese and your parish. Pray for the pope, for your bishop, for your pastor—by name. Pray for effective reform.

- Pray for those who suffer for the Faith: for Christians who are persecuted in the Middle East, those who are targeted in Africa, those whose religious freedoms are curtailed by governments in Asia.

- Pray for those who do not have the Faith, who have not heard the Gospel message or have not properly understood it. Pray for missionary works and evangelists—and identify with them, since we are all members of the same "team."

- Pray for Catholics who are no longer practicing their faith, for the disaffected, the alienated, the dissidents. Pray for their return.

DON'T

- Be content with sloppy liturgy, inappropriate liturgical music, and banal homilies. (Do find a parish church where you can be inspired.)

- Accept spurious assertions that the religious-education program is rigorous, or that spiritual life at the parish is "vibrant" when you know better. (Do contradict silly claims.)

- Sit through (or lead!) a marriage-preparation program that does not accentuate the distinctive Catholic teaching on the meaning of marriage. If the program doesn't tackle the topic of contraception, it's not honest.

- Attend the wedding of a same-sex couple, or of friends who have already been married (and have not received an annulment). You are being asked to serve as a witness; if you don't believe that a real marriage is taking place, you can't be a witness to it. Your refusal to attend may cause real pain, even to you yourself. That's a price you should pay for your integrity in the Faith.

DO

- Help people who are in need. Give your money *and your time*. Find ways to be *personally* involved with people who need help: in soup kitchens, shelters, clinics, etc.

- Bear in mind that sometimes the people in greatest need are the lonely. Visit hospitals or nursing homes; volunteer at a hospice.

- Be aware of friends and neighbors who may be having troubles. Sometimes people who are in need are reluctant to ask for help. Ask them if there's anything you can do. (Don't press if they decline the offer, but make sure they know they can call on you if they change their minds.)

- Contribute generously to worthy causes, such as the pro-life movement. Choose a few charities in which you have full confidence. Choose causes where your donations will make a difference; don't focus on fashionable charities. Be a consistent supporter and send appropriate advice and encouragement along with your checks. Think about joining the organization's board.

DON'T

- Contribute to any "Catholic" institution— school, college, hospital, or charity—that does not proudly uphold its Catholic identity.

- Send your children to parochial schools that compromise or endanger their faith by teaching something different from Church doctrine.
- Support secular charities that are involved *in any way* with abortion, coercive family planning, the distribution of contraceptives, the promotion of homosexuality, or other immoral public causes.
- Participate in annual diocesan appeals, or other Church fundraising drives, if some of the pooled funds will be used for purposes you cannot endorse. Earmark your donations for specific purposes.

DO

- Encourage good Catholic leaders. Find occasions to thank your pastor for good homilies or for taking a firm stand on some local issue. (If you can never find an occasion to thank your pastor, think about finding a new parish.)
- Find a good parish. Make sacrifices if necessary to be somewhere where you—and especially your children—will be strengthened and nurtured spiritually. It's awfully difficult to fight the spiritual battles alone; find a source of support.
- Seek out friends who share your Catholic faith. Spend time with them—perhaps on Sunday afternoons? Let your children play together; when they're teenagers, they will form a healthy support group for each other.

- Set up a program for Eucharistic Adoration at your parish. Don't just ask your pastor to do it; volunteer to coordinate the effort. Recruit people to spend one hour a week with our Eucharistic Lord. Count on this: the results will astonish you.
- If you see something wrong—liturgical abuse, improper behavior, unorthodox teaching—say something. Talk first to the individual involved, then to the pastor, then to the bishop, if necessary, to the apostolic nuncio. Be polite but persistent.

DON'T

- Be known as someone who always has a complaint. Be positive whenever possible.
- "Ambush" the bishop at a social gathering. If you have a serious issue to discuss, make an appointment or write to him. Many bishops now correspond by email as well. Again, be persistent. You have a right to a hearing; if you aren't given an appointment promptly, ask again. And again.
- Give priests (or anyone else) new tasks without offering to help. Good priests are already busy; lazy priests are . . . well, lazy. Make it easy for the priest to say yes.
- Scold. There is a legitimate role in the Christian community for "fraternal correction"—for letting a fellow Christian know that he has done something wrong. But out of prudence, the Church traditionally teaches that a fraternal correction should be offered only when there is a reasonable

expectation that it will be taken the right way. Even if you're right, you could make things worse. When in doubt, talk to a trusted friend—ideally, your spiritual director—before taking action.

DO

- Invite people to visit your church. If the subject comes up naturally in conversation (or if you can bring it up without being awkward), tell friends about your faith. Ask them if they've ever been interested in Catholicism.

- Foster devotions in your own home, in your parish, and among your friends. Gather for the Rosary. Make pilgrimages. Have special dinners to celebrate the feasts of your favorite saints. Invite your friends and encourage them to follow your lead in hosting such get-togethers.

- Celebrate the major *and minor* feast days. Observe the Ember Days. Make the effort to live by the rhythm of the Church's liturgical calendar. If possible, pray at least part of the Liturgy of the Hours—remember that this is part of the Church's official liturgy.

- Take a deep plunge into the treasury of our Catholic heritage. Read Dante. Sing Palestrina. Recite "Lepanto." Stage a Christmas pageant.

- Make a point of greeting new people who show up at your parish. Invite them to a barbeque. Welcome them into your circle of friends and introduce them into your way of celebrating the joys of

Catholic life. You'll find that many people want to be part of that circle; the Faith is contagious.

- Then stand back, keep praying, and prepare for the Catholic revival.

Notes

1   https://www.thebostonpilot.com/article.asp?ID=1833
    42&utm_source=dlvr.it&utm_medium=twitter
2   http://w2.vatican.va/content/paul-vi/it/homilies/1972/
    documents/hf_p-vi_hom_19720629.html
3   http://www.ncregister.com/blog/joseph-pronechen/
    fulton-sheen-answers-for-a-christendom-crisis
4   This and other statements by Pope Francis cited
    within the text were all reported in multiple news
    outlets, and the original source would in many cases
    be either the Vatican Press Office http://www.vatican.
    va/news_services/press/index.htm) or the Vatican
    News Service (https://www.vaticannews.va/en.html).
5   https://www.catholicnewsagency.com/news/cardinal-
    omalley-popes-words-a-source-of-great-pain-for-
    abuse-survivors-99063
6   https://apnews.com/07e48f9e01c54ec496397f68bea5d30a
7   https://www.apnews.com/01983501d40d47a4aa7
    a32b6afb70661
8   https://www.nytimes.com/2018/04/09/world/europe/
    pope-francis-migrants-abortion.html
9   Earlier versions of this book, following multiple media

reports on the matter, indicated that Apuron had been convicted of sexual abuse by the Vatican Tribunal. All reports lead to that conclusion, and his successor has been unequivocal in referring to the abuse committed by his predecessor. The Vatican statement, however, at the conclusion of the trial was woefully unclear, not that he was convicted, as he was, but concerning the exact nature of the crimes of which he was convicted. The phrase "certain charges" was used. The lack of clarity on the part of the Vatican in this matter has led to no small amount of confusion, perhaps yet another indication that problems remain when it comes to transparency in this area. —Ed.

10 https://archny.org/cardinalmccarrick

11 https://archny.org/statement-of-cardinal-theodore-mccarrick

12 http://www.ncregister.com/daily-news/honduran-seminarians-allege-widespread-homosexual-misconduct

13 https://www.bostoncatholic.org/Utility/News-And-Press/Content.aspx?id=34865

14 https://nypost.com/2018/08/27/the-catholic-abuse-scandal-now-leads-all-the-to-way-the-vatican/

15 https://www.catholicnewsagency.com/news/former-nunciature-official-vigano-said-the-truth-38319

16 https://www.nbcchicago.com/news/local/cardinal-cupich-pope-bigger-agenda_Chicago-491855581.html

17 http://www.usccb.org/news/2018/18-143.cfm

18 https://www.catholicnewsagency.com/news/cardinal-dinardo-calls-meeting-with-pope-lengthy-fruitful-20709

19 https://www.getreligion.org/getreligion/2018/6/21/the-scandal-of-cardinal-mccarrick-and-why-no-major-media-outed-him

20 http://www.catholicherald.co.uk/news/2018/02/23/
diocese-says-cardinal-nighty-night-baby-tweet-was-
meant-for-sister/

21 https://www.catholicculture.org/commentary/otr.
cfm?id=2765

22 http://www.cccb.ca/site/eng/media-room/archives/
media-releases/2006/2364-address-of-cardinal-
theodore-mccarrick-to-the-plenary-assembly-of-the-
cccb-17-october-2006

23 https://www.firstthings.com/web-exclusives/2014/04/
clearing-the-waters

24 https://www.reuters.com/article/us-vatican-bank-
investigation/arrested-vatican-prelate-lived-lush-life-
in-hometown-idUSBRE96308S20130704

25 http://www.ncregister.com/daily-news/consecrated-
life-today-enjoying-good-health-archbishop-
affirms#ixzz2sGzLLhjh

26 https://www.catholicculture.org/culture/library/view.
cfm?id=8889

27 https://www.catholicnewsagency.com/news/women_
religious_leadership_conference_faces_investigation_
for_continued_problems

28 https://www.catholicculture.org/culture/library/view.
cfm?id=10229

29 https://www.catholicculture.org/news/headlines/
index.cfm?storyid=24640

30 https://in.reuters.com/article/usa-contraception-
georgetown/feature-us-rule-highlights-catholic-tensions-
over-contraception-idINL2E8IVGX720120801

31 His Humble Servant: Sister M. Pascalina Lehnert's
Memoirs of Her Years of Service to Eugenio Pacelli,
Pope Pius XII, p. 150, Saint Augustine's Press, tr.

Susan Johnson 2014

32 https://zenit.org/articles/cardinal-ratzinger-tells-why-many-misperceive-christianity/

33 https://www.firstthings.com/article/2013/10/the-impossibility-of-secular-society

34 https://www.americamagazine.org/content/all-things/catholic-pagan-10-questions-camille-paglia

35 https://www.wsj.com/articles/SB1000142405270230 381650457731180082127018

36 https://www.americamagazine.org/faith/2013/09/30/big-heart-open-god-interview-pope-francis

37 http://w2.vatican.va/content/benedict-xvi/en/speeches/2008/april/documents/hf_ben-xvi_spe_20080416_response-bishops.html

38 https://www.firstthings.com/article/2014/03/this-time-will-not-be-the-same

39 http://w2.vatican.va/content/pius-x/en/encyclicals/documents/hf_p-x_enc_19070908_pascendi-dominici-gregis.html Art. 3.

40 https://zenit.org/articles/cardinal-parolin-comments-on-holy-see-republic-of-china-agreement/

41 https://laciviltacattolica.com/the-agreement-between-china-and-the-holy-see/

42 http://w2.vatican.va/content/leo-xiii/en/encyclicals/documents/hf_l-xiii_enc_10011890_sapientiae-christianae.html

43 http://www.orthodoxytoday.org/articles/Solhenitsyn Lies.php

Sources and Suggestions
for Further Reading

Von Balthasar, Hans Urs. *Theo-Drama: Theological Dramatic Theory*. San Francisco: Ignatius Press, 1993.

Bonhoeffer, Dietrich, *The Cost of Discipleship*. Touchstone, 1995 edition.

Pope Benedict XVI, (tr. Adrian J. Walker). *Jesus of Nazareth: From the Baptism in the Jordan to the Transfiguration*. San Francisco: Ignatius Press, 2007.

Pope Benedict XVI, (tr. Adrian J. Walker). *Jesus of Nazareth: The Infancy Narratives*. San Francisco: Ignatius Press, 2012.

Pope Benedict XVI, (tr. Adrian J. Walker). *Jesus of Nazareth: Holy Week: From the Entrance Into Jerusalem To The Resurrection*. San Francisco: Ignatius Press, 2011.

Carlin, David. *The Decline and Fall of the Catholic Church in America*. Manchester: Sophia Institute Press, 2013.

The Selected Letters of Willa Cather, (ed. Jewell, Andrew and Janice Stout). New York: Alfred A. Knopf, 2013.

Conyers, A.J. *The Long Truce: How Toleration Made the World Safe for Power and Profit, 2ⁿᵈ ed.* Dallas: Spence Publishing, 2001.

Day, Dorothy. *The Long Loneliness: The Autobiography of the Legendary Catholic Social Activist.* San Francisco: HarperOne, (2009 edition).

Day, Thomas. *Why Catholics Can't Sing: The Culture of Catholicism and the Triumph of Bad Taste.* New York: The Crossroad Publishing Company, 1990.

Francis Cardinal George. *God in Action: How Faith in God Can Address the Challenges of the World.* Image, 2011.

von Hildebrand, Dietrich, (tr. John Crosby & Fred Teichert). *The Devastated Vineyard.* Chicago: Franciscan Herald Press, 1973.

Hitchcock, James. *History of the Catholic Church: From the Apostolic Age to the Third Millennium.* San Francisco: Ignatius Press, 2012.

Lawler, Philip F. *When Faith Goes Viral: 11 Success Stories of the New Evangelization from Alabama to Vladivostok.* New York: The Crossroad Publishing Company, 2013.

Lehnert, Sister M. Pascalina, (tr. Susan Johnson). *Sister M. Pascalina Lehnert's Memoirs of Her Years of Service to Eugenio Pacelli, Pope Pius XII.* South Bend: Saint Augustine's Press, 2014.

Martin, Ralph. *Will Many Be Saved? What Vatican II Actually Teaches and Its Implications for the New Evangelization.* Grand Rapids: Eerdmans, 2012.

Ratzinger, Joseph Cardinal. *Faith and the Future*. San Francisco: Ignatius Press, 2009.

Sarah, Robert Cardinal and Nicholas Diat. *God or Nothing: A Conversation on Faith*. San Francisco: Ignatius Press, 2015.

Saward, John, *The Beauty of Holiness and the Holiness of Beauty: Art, Sanctity, and the Truth of Catholicism*. San Francisco: Ignatius Press, 1997.

Sheed, Francis Joseph. *Christ in Eclipse, A Clinical Study of the Good Christian*. Kansas City: Andrews McMeel, 1978.

Weigel, George. *Evangelical Catholicism: Deep Reform in the 21st-Century Church*. New York: Basic Books, 2014.

About the Author

Philip F. Lawler, the founder of the Catholic World News service, is the author of *The Faithful Departed*, which the late Father Richard Neuhaus described in 2008 as "the best book-length treatment of the sex abuse crisis, its origins and larger implications, published to date." More recently he wrote *Lost Shepherd*, a critical analysis of Pope Francis's leadership. With *The Smoke of Satan*, he completes his analysis of the crisis of confidence in the Church and explains how an engaged and determined laity can help trigger worldwide Catholic revival.

Made in the USA
Middletown, DE
18 November 2018